THE COMPLETE TAPAS COOKBOOK

2 Books in 1: 140 Recipes For Spanish Traditional Food

Emma Yang
Maki Blanc

TAPAS
COOKBOOK

70 Easy Recipes For
Traditional Food From Spain

Emma Yang

© **Copyright 2021 by (Emma Yang) - All rights reserved.**

This document is geared towards providing exact and reliable information in regards to the topic and issue covered. The publication is sold with the idea that the publisher is not required to render accounting, officially permitted, or otherwise, qualified services. If advice is necessary, legal or professional, a practiced individual in the profession should be ordered.

- From a Declaration of Principles which was accepted and approved equally by a Committee of the American Bar Association and a Committee of Publishers and Associations.

It is not legal in any way to reproduce, duplicate, or transmit any part of this document in either electronic means or in printed format. Recording of this publication is strictly prohibited and any storage of this document is not allowed unless with written permission from the publisher. All rights reserved.

The information provided herein is stated to be truthful and consistent, in that any liability, in terms of inattention or otherwise, by any usage or abuse of any policies, processes, or directions contained within is the solitary and utter responsibility of the recipient reader. Under no circumstances will any legal responsibility or blame be held against the publisher for any reparation, damages, or monetary loss due to the information herein, either directly or indirectly.

Respective authors own all copyrights not held by the publisher.

The information herein is offered for informational purposes solely, and is universal as so. The presentation of the information is without contract or any type of guarantee assurance.

The trademarks that are used are without any consent, and the publication of the trademark is without permission or backing by the trademark owner. All trademarks and brands within this book are for clarifying purposes only and are the owned by the owners themselves, not affiliated with this document.

Contents

INTRODUCTION 13

CHAPTER 1: SPANISH FOOD AT A GLANCE 15

1.1 History of Spanish Cuisine..15

1.2 History of Traditional Spanish Dishes 16

1.3 Health Benefits of Spanish Food...17

1.4 Key Ingredients for Preparing Spanish Food at Home..........17

CHAPTER 2: TAPAS BREAKFAST AND APPETIZER RECIPES 19

2.1 Veggie Spanish-style Chorizo Omelets....................................19

2.2 Mushroom, Tomato & Polenta Tapas......................................20

2.3 Mediterranean Olive Toss..21

2.4 Easy Tomato Gazpacho Recipe...22

2.5 Spanish Churros and Chocolate 23

2.6 Mediterranean Wrap 25

2.7 20-Minute Couscous Recipe with Shrimp and Chorizo 26

2.8 Spanish Tapas Toast with Escalivada.......................................27

2.9 Pan con Tomate 28

2.10 Zucchini Tapas Omelet 29

2.11 Basque Breakfast Sandwich...30

2.12 Spanish Churros and Chocolate...31

5

2.13 Mini Spanish Omelets 32

CHAPTER 3: TAPAS SNACK, SOUPS, SALADS RECIPES 34

3.1 Veggie Loaded Spanish Style Rice 34

3.2 Tofu and Olive Tapas 35

3.3 Patatas Bravas 36

3.4 Mediterranean Seafood Stew 38

3.5 Spanish Orange & Olive Salad 39

3.6 Mediterranean-Style Steamed Clams Recipe 41

3.7 Avocado and Tuna Tapas 42

3.8 Fish Tapas 43

3.9 Garlic Soup with Egg and Croutons 44

3.10 Spanish Tapas-Style Green Pepper 45

3.11 Magdalenas: Spanish Lemon Cupcakes 46

3.12 Cucumber Tapas 47

CHAPTER 4: TAPAS LUNCH AND DINNER RECIPES .49

4.1 Spanish Style Rice 49

4.2 Mediterranean Basa Stew & Sunny Aioli 50

4.3 25-Minute Shrimp and Chorizo 52

4.4 Spanish Rice Dinner 53

4.5 Spicy Crab Salad Tapas 54

4.6 Pulpo Gallego: A Galician-Style Octopus Tapas 56

4.7 Roasted Vegetable Tapas 57

4.8 Chicken Tapas with Romesco Sauce 58

4.9 Fried Chorizo with Chick Peas and Tomatoes 60

4.10 Boquerones Al Limon 61

4.11 Spanish Tapas Platter 62

4.12 Catalan Fig Tapas 63

4.13 Quick and Easy Paella 64

4.14 Tapas & Pinchos Vegetarian 65

CHAPTER 5: VEGETARIAN TAPAS RECIPES 68

5.1 Spanish Vegan Paella 68

5.2 Smoked Vegetarian Spanish Rice Recipe 69

5.3 Champinones Spanish Garlic Mushrooms 70

5.4 Spanish Vegetarian Tapas 71

5.5 Spanish Vegetarian Stew 73

5.6 Spanish Tapas-Inspired Mussels 74

5.7 Tapas Style Garlic Mushrooms 75

5.8 Spanish Rice Skillet Meal 76

5.9 Mediterranean Baked Tapas 77

5.10 Chorizo and Potato Tapas 78

CHAPTER 6: CLASSIC SPANISH DISHES 80

6.1 Mediterranean Skillet Chicken with Bulgur Paella, Carrots
.... 80

6.2 One Pan Spanish Chicken and Rice Recipe with Chorizo ...82

6.3 Spanish Mixed Green Salad...84

6.4 Saucy Spanish Chicken with Green Olives 85

6.5 Pisto...86

6.6 Easy Seafood Paella Recipe..87

6.7 Gambas al Ajillo 88

6.8 Easy Spanish Tortilla Recipe..89

6.9 Easy Spanish Garlic Soup..90

6.10 Rustic Spanish Chicken Casserole......................................92

6.11 Summer Spanish Salad 93

6.12 Spanish Tuna and Potato Salad Recipe 94

6.13 Spanish Style Albondigas 95

6.14 Pontevedra-Style Spanish Chicken....................................97

6.15 Spanish Cold Tomato Soup...98

6.16 Spicy Spanish Meatballs..99

6.17 Sizzling Spanish Garlic Prawns 100

6.18 Super Tasty Spanish Roast Chicken...............................101

6.19 Spanish-Inspired Tomato Salad 102

6.20 Fruity Spanish Tapas...103

CONCLUSION...105

CHAPTER 1: GETTING STARTED WITH SPANISH FOOD
....111

1.1 History of Spanish Food 111

1.2 History of Traditional Dishes from Spain 112

1.3 Health Benefits of Spanish Food 113

1.4 Preparing Ingredients for Spanish Dishes 115

CHAPTER 2: TAPAS BREAKFAST, SNACKS, AND APPETIZERS 117

2.1 Fried Chorizo with Chick Peas and Tomatoes 117

2.2 Boquerones Al Limon 118

2.3 Spanish Churros and Chocolate 119

2.4 Basque Breakfast Sandwich 120

2.5 Spicy Crab Salad Tapas 121

2.6 Mini Spanish Omelets 123

2.7 Zucchini Tapas Omelet 125

2.8 Roasted Vegetable Tapas 126

2.9 Pan con Tomate 128

2.10 Cucumber Tapas 129

2.11 Spanish Tapas Platter 130

2.12 Magdalenas: Spanish Lemon Cupcakes 131

2.13 Pulpo Gallego: A Galician-Style Octopus Tapas 132

2.14 Spanish Tapas Toast with Escalivada 134

CHAPTER 3: TAPAS LUNCH, SOUPS AND SALAD 135

3.1 Easy Spanish Garlic Soup 135

3.2 Garlic Soup with Egg and Croutons 136

3.3 Salmorejo (Spanish Cold Tomato Soup) 137

3.4 Chorizo and Potato Tapas 138

3.5 Spanish Tapas-Style Green Pepper 140

3.6 Pontevedra-Style Spanish Chicken 140

3.7 Mediterranean Baked Tapas 141

3.8 Chicken Tapas with Romesco Sauce 142

3.9 Spicy Spanish Meatballs 143

3.10 Spanish One-Pan Chicken with Chorizo and Bell Peppers 145

3.11 Sizzling Spanish Garlic Prawns 147

3.12 Super Tasty Spanish Roast Chicken 148

3.13 Spanish Mixed Green Salad 149

3.14 Spanish-Inspired Tomato Salad 150

CHAPTER 4: TAPAS DINNER AND DESSERTS 152

4.1 Spanish Rice Dinner 152

4.2 Shrimp and Chorizo Tapas 153

4.3 Tapas Style Garlic Mushrooms 154

4.4 Spicy Shrimp Tapas 155

4.5 Fruity Spanish Tapas 156

4.6 Spanish Tapas-Inspired Mussels 157

4.7 Spanish-Style Chicken with Mushrooms 158

4.8 Avocado and Tuna Tapas 159

4.9 Fish Tapas 160

4.10 Spanish Rice Skillet Meal 162

4.11 Champinones Spanish Garlic Mushrooms 163

4.12 Catalan Fig Tapas 164

4.13 Quick and Easy Paella 165

CHAPTER 5: CLASSIC SPANISH DISHES 167

5.1 Spanish Style Albondigas 167

5.2 Mediterranean Basa Stew & Sunny Aioli 169

5.3 Mediterranean Olive Toss 170

5.4 Spanish Orange & Olive Salad 171

5.5 Pisto (Spanish Vegetable Stew) 173

5.6 Mediterranean Skillet Chicken with Bulgur Paella, Carrots 174

5.7 Rustic Spanish Chicken Casserole 177

5.8 Mediterranean Seafood Stew 178

5.9 Saucy Spanish Chicken with Green Olives 179

5.10 Summer Spanish Salad 181

5.11 Rice Spanish Vegetables Recipe 182

5.12 Mediterranean Wrap 184

5.13 Easy Tomato Gazpacho Recipe 185

5.14 Spanish Tuna and Potato Salad Recipe 186

5.15 Easy Seafood Paella Recipe 188

5.16 One Pan Spanish Chicken and Rice Recipe with Chorizo 189

5.17 20-Minute Couscous Recipe with Shrimp and Chorizo **191**

5.18 Gambas al Ajillo **192**

5.19 Mediterranean-Style Steamed Clams Recipe **193**

5.20 Easy Spanish Tortilla Recipe **195**

CHAPTER 6: TAPAS VEGETARIAN RECIPES **197**

6.1 Spanish Vegetarian Stew **197**

6.2 Spanish Vegan Paella **198**

6.3 Tofu and Olive Tapas **199**

6.4 Veggie Loaded Spanish Style Rice **202**

6.5 Veggie Spanish-style Chorizo Omelets **203**

6.6 Smoked Vegetarian Spanish Rice Recipe **204**

6.7 Tapas & Pinchos Vegetarian **206**

6.8 Spanish Vegetarian Tapas **207**

6.9 Patatas Bravas **209**

6.10 Mushroom, Polenta & Tomato Tapas **210**

CONCLUSION 212

Introduction

Tapas are far more advanced nowadays. Tapas include everything from small olive sauces to intricate culinary skills. There are also tapas competitions to see who can make the best versions! Tapas has evolved to include briny mussels, cherry tomatoes, fried cod, and other delicacies. As the tapas tradition in Spain expands, tapas bars have grown to include small plates rather than just quick bites. Tapas have become more creative in recent years, and there are now various recipes to try. Tapas was always about using new, in-season Mediterranean products as well as traditional Spanish culinary delights. That is what you will be on the lookout for. Do not be put off by the presence of canned food in restaurants. Spain is described as having some of the finest packaged seafood on the earth. Sardines, clams, oysters, and other seafood are common in Spanish cuisine, do not be afraid to try them. Anything else would pale in comparison to the tapas culture of Spain.

To begin with, a "tapa" is merely a small serving of food. Tapas can be eaten in a variety of ways. The most popular origin story for tapas is that they began as tiny slices of meats or toast served in cafes as a way for drinkers to keep flies away from their beverages. The Spanish word tapas means "to cover." Gradually, the tiny bar snack became just as important as the beverages. They began to become more elaborate as well. Tapas describes the way food is served rather than individual dishes. Tapas have spread across Spain and have become an important part of their culture, as tapas have developed alongside Spanish food culture.

Tapas are divided into three categories: pinchos, cosas de picar, and cazuelas. Tiny foods such as artichokes and Jamon are known as Cosas de picar.

Pinchos are tapas that come with a chopstick, such as a slice of Spain flatbread fixed to a loaf of toast with a toothpick. Cazuelas are specialty pizzas of food with salsa and a bit more material, such as grilled shrimp, sausages, or even a whole Spanish flatbread. Spain is a nation with a long and diverse coastline. It is the ruler of a Mediterranean Ocean and North Atlantic territory. As a result, a ton of fish appears on Spanish lists. The anchovy, a sweetness full of Omega-3 fats, Vitamin b, magnesium, and phosphorus, is most common. Many anchovies are wrapped in salt, which can be washed away with water.

"Tapas Cookbook" has a wide range of Tapas and Spanish recipes with different ingredients and methods. It has six chapters based on Breakfast, snack, lunch, dinner, salad, soups, and vegetarian recipes. All recipes with lots of health benefits are here. Try these recipes and make your meal more delightful and flavorful.

Chapter 1: Spanish Food at a Glance

Food material from the area's rugged terrain is emphasized in Spanish cuisine. Small plates of high-quality products, as well as salmon and veggies, are popular. While rich foods like Iberico ham and serrano ham are available, Spain also offers various lighter and healthy options. There is no such thing as a calorie-restricted plan in Spain. The Spanish place a premium on spending time with family and friends while still staying physically involved. It's an integral part of their everyday routine and a tradition as significant as football. Since food is considered sacred and intended to be appreciated, the Spanish do not limit themselves to calorie counting, fatty grams, or fructose intake to determine moderation.

1.1 History of Spanish Cuisine

Spain's place, especially in the Atlantic Ocean and the Mediterranean Sea, has influenced its cuisine. In traditional Spanish recipes, salmon is abundant and common. The several foreign locations that Spain once invaded have also had a strong influence on Traditional dishes. For example, Arabic crops such as grain, cocoa beans, auberge, peanuts, and lemon are frequently used in Spanish cuisine. Spain ruled several parts of South America during the arrival of the new era. They finally brought a range of foods from South America, including onions, tomatoes, peas, and cocoa. At the period, Spanish cuisine was still evolving, incorporating products from all over the world. The Spanish were using tomatoes in their cuisine for a long time. Spain has a long agricultural history that includes a diverse variety of nutrients.

It is one of the world's leading suppliers of grape and artichokes, in general. These ingredients are used in the production of two of Spain's most popular products: liquor and olives. Spanish cuisine is still developing today, and it is one of the pioneers in developing a healthy balanced diet.

1.2 History of Traditional Spanish Dishes

Traditional Spanish food is simple, unpretentious food made with locally sourced ingredients or staple crops in the area. Mountains pass through Spain in many ways, creating natural access barriers and rendering transportation impossible until the second half of the twentieth century. This is only one of the factors why cooking varies so much from place to place. The other is that Spain was formed by the union of several independent kingdoms with its customs. Cocoas, in general, are one of those products that have influenced global eating habits. This snack became so famous around the world due to Spain's healthy appetite. Plus, they mixed it with other flavors such delicacies as caramel con churros and Atletico favorite. Most dishes are now cooked using the same techniques and products as they had been two or three centuries ago. Like the Romans, the Arabs who invaded and lived in Spain for over eight hundred years made significant contributions to Traditional dishes, as seen in many dishes. Other dishes arose as a result of American and European factors and were then adjusted to Spanish preferences. A few things have not changed: The food in Spain is clean, plentiful, and flavorful, and the Spaniards adore it.

1.3 Health Benefits of Spanish Food

Its world-famous Mediterranean diet emphasizes a high intake of vegetables, berries, peanuts, grains, and fish, as well as plenty of olive oil, reasonable dairy intake, and a low intake of red meat. At meals, it is often common to drink that little wine professionally. The Spanish food is heart-healthy, which may clarify why Spain has lower heart disease rates. The diet can help with weight loss comfortably due to its emphasis on the whole, healthy produce. It's not for a quick fix, but it's a good eating habit to develop long-term results. The Spanish eating healthy style helps avoid gestational diabetes and is ideal for managing and regulating blood sugar levels. Certain aspects of the diet, such as its high anti-inflammatory omega-3 fats, seem to help alleviate RA symptoms. Lentils provide 63 percent of your daily soluble fiber needs in just one cup. This aids in the regulation of blood sugar, metabolism, and losing weight. Lentils often include phosphorus and magnesium, all of which are beneficial to cardiovascular health. Olives are high in monounsaturated fats, which lower cardiovascular disease risk and increase HDL cholesterol levels. Olives do have anti-inflammatory and antioxidant activities, which means they can help prevent diseases and cancers.

1.4 Key Ingredients for Preparing Spanish Food at Home

Beef, pork, and lamb are all traditional cuts of meat that can be roasted, fried over charcoal, or sautéed in a sauce. Cloves, tomatoes, and herbs like thyme, cardamom, and rosemary are all used, but garlic is used more than others. Ham, or jamón in Spanish, is a valued delicacy.

Spaniards are passionate about their ham and would pay a premium for the best. Eggs are consumed regularly, whether fried, mashed potatoes, or in a Spanish omelet known as a tortilla Espaola. Almonds, walnuts, and hazelnuts are among Spain's main exports. Desserts made with almonds and milk are very popular. In view of food, Spain is still one of the most popular nations in the world. Spain has evolved into one of the world's first and most influential "fusion" delicacies.

Chapter 2: Tapas Breakfast and Appetizer Recipes

2.1 Veggie Spanish-style Chorizo Omelets

Cooking Time: 55 minutes

Serving Size: 8

Ingredients:

For the Roasted Vegetables

- 2 tablespoon olive oil
- Salt and pepper to taste
- 2 medium potatoes
- ¾ teaspoon smoky BBQ seasoning
- 2 medium red onions
- 1 red pepper

For the Omelet

- 8 yolk eggs

For the Veggie Chorizo

- 1 teaspoon olive oil
- 8 shroom does

Method:

1. Heat the oven to 220 degrees Celsius.
2. Stir the chicken pieces, peppers, sliders, and onions with the smoky spices and vegetable oil.
3. Fry the potato for 25-30 minutes, or till they have hardened.
4. Heat the chorizo-style shroomdogs over the last fifteen minutes of the veggies frying.

5. Remove the veggies from the oven until they are finished.
6. Slowly transfer the egg mixture into the pan.
7. Season the eggs with salt and black pepper to taste, then uniformly distribute the leftover sausage strips and veggies on top.

2.2 Mushroom, Tomato & Polenta Tapas

Cooking Time: 30 minutes

Serving Size: 4

Ingredients:

- 4 sundried tomatoes
- Salt & pepper
- 1 clove garlic
- A small lump of parmesan
- 400g polenta
- Parsley
- A lug of olive oil
- 8 mushrooms
- 50g feta cheese
- 3 big tomatoes

Method:

1. Preheat the grill to 200 degrees Celsius.
2. Heat the polenta as per the package directions.
3. Cut the tomatoes into rounds.
4. Remove the stems and wash the mushrooms with a towel.

5. Toss the vegetables and mushrooms in the seasoning.
6. To cook and smooth the vegetables and mushrooms, position them under the barbecue in the oven.
7. Rub the polenta round with olive oil and barbecue them on a stovetop grill, rotating to build nice lines from both ends.
8. To arrange, start with the polenta square, then a tomato slice, and finally a mushroom.

2.3 Mediterranean Olive Toss

Cooking Time: 45 minutes

Serving Size: 8

Ingredients:
- 2 cups spinach leaves
- ½ cup feta cheese
- 7 pickled red peppers
- ¼ cup Kalamata olives
- 1 package penne pasta
- 4 large cloves of garlic
- 1 (8 ounces) jar artichoke
- ⅓ cup olive oil

Method:
1. Fill a large pot halfway with liquid and bring to the boil, lightly toasted.
2. Return to a boil after adding the penne.
3. Heat pasta for ten minutes, covered, then rinse.

4. In a large skillet over medium heat, heat the olive oil on moderate heat and cook and mix garlic once aromatic, around 30 seconds.
5. Stir to combine flavors 5 minutes after adding the pine nuts, tomatoes, and artichokes to the skillet.
6. Remove from the heat and stir in the penne pasta until well combined; toss the pasta mixture gently with the feta cheese.

2.4 Easy Tomato Gazpacho Recipe

Cooking Time: 15 minutes

Serving Size: 6

Ingredients:

- A small handful of mint leaves
- Small cilantro leaves
- 5 slices stale artisan bread
- 1 teaspoon cayenne pepper
- Pinch sugar
- Water
- Salt and pepper
- ½ teaspoon cumin
- 5 large ripe tomatoes
- Olive oil
- 2 tablespoon sherry vinegar
- ½ English cucumber
- 2 green onions
- 2 garlic cloves

- 1 green pepper
- 1 celery stalk

Method:

1. In a pan, combine the bread slices and ½ cup of water.
2. Remove the tops of the tomatoes.
3. Combine the tomatoes, carrots, fennel, green beans, fresh basil, and garlic in a big blender or food processor.
4. Place the soaking bread on top.
5. Pour ½ cup olive oil and sherry wine into a mixing bowl.
6. If the gazpacho is too thick, add more water and mix again until consistency is right.
7. Fill a glass beaker or wide canning jar with the mixture.
8. Cover tightly with plastic wrap and place in the refrigerator to cool.
9. Offer the gazpacho a short swirl before transferring it to serving bowls or small glasses.

2.5 Spanish Churros and Chocolate

Cooking Time: 45 minutes

Serving Size: 14

Ingredients:

For the Cinnamon Sugar

- 2 tablespoons granulated sugar
- 1 teaspoon cinnamon

For the Chocolate Sauce
- 1 cup semisweet chocolate
- 1 ¼ cups heavy cream

For the Churros Dough
- 1 cup all-purpose flour
- Vegetable oil
- ½ teaspoon kosher salt
- 2 tablespoons vegetable oil
- 2½ tablespoons sugar
- 1 cup water

Method:
1. Mix the sugars and spices in a small bowl and stir to blend.
2. Add the cream to a pot over medium heat. Get it to a low simmer.
3. Put the cocoa in a heatproof cup, add the hot butter over it, and cover the bucket in cling film.
4. Combine the sugar, salt, and soybean oil in a mixing bowl.
5. Get the water to a boil, then turn off the steam.
6. Mix in the flour until it creates a creamy sauce.
7. In a skillet, add the oil to 375°F over moderate flame.
8. Deep-fry for four minutes, or until golden, nicely browned.
9. Toss with the cinnamon and sugar right away.
10. With the white chocolate, serve hot or at ambient temperature.

2.6 Mediterranean Wrap

Cooking Time: 10 minutes
Serving Size: 1
Ingredients:

- 2 tablespoons basil pesto
- 1-2 tablespoons feta cheese
- ¼ cup rotisserie chicken
- 3 tablespoons tomatoes
- 1 cow cheese wedge
- ½ cup greens lettuce
- 1 tortilla wrap

Method:

1. Place the tortilla on a flat surface and scatter the Cow cheesy wedge down the middle.
2. Insert the mixed greens just to the side of the cheese.
3. Cover with the meat, sun-dried vegetables, and pesto, spooned on top and softly spread.
4. Over the risotto, break the gruyere cheese.
5. Fold the upper part of the tortilla inwards somewhat, then roll it up tightly.
6. Break the wrap in half with a sharp knife and eat right away!

2.7 20-Minute Couscous Recipe with Shrimp and Chorizo

Cooking Time: 25 minutes

Serving Size: 6

Ingredients:

- Boiling water
- 1 cup fresh parsley
- 1.5 lb. large shrimp
- 1 ¼ cup couscous
- 1 ¼ teaspoon ground cumin
- Salt
- 1 ¼ teaspoon turmeric
- 1 ¼ teaspoon paprika
- 6 oz. hard Spanish Chorizo
- 3 garlic cloves
- 2 jalapeno peppers
- 1 small yellow onion
- Extra virgin olive

Method:

1. Heat a small amount of vegetable oil in a large frying pan.
2. Heat the Chorizo sausage rolls until they are crisp.
3. Remove from the heat and clean on towels.
4. Add the garlic, onions, and habanero to the boiling pot and cook till the vegetables are transparent.

5. Now insert the seasoning and mix for a few seconds before adding the shrimp.
6. Heat the shrimp for approximately 3 minutes on moderate flame.
7. In the meantime, bring 2 ½ cups of water to a boil.
8. Transfer the couscous, little more vegetable oil, a pinch of salt, and the hot oil to the frying pan with the Chorizo.
9. Allow for five minutes of resting time. Remove the cover and add the fresh parsley.
10. Enjoy by moving to serve pots.

2.8 Spanish Tapas Toast with Escalivada

Cooking Time: 15 minutes

Serving Size: 4

Ingredients:
- Flat-leaf parsley
- Sea salt
- 80g soft goat's cheese
- 1 slice Serrano ham
- ½ jar of Escalivada
- Green olives
- Extra virgin olive oil
- 1 large bruschetta bread

Method:
1. After toasting one side of the bruschetta crust, sprinkle the uncooked side with olive oil.
2. Drain the escalivada with a fork.

3. Place the whole or doubled olives on top, then sprinkle the goat's cheese on top.
4. Put the toast back under the flame.
5. Blow the Spicy salami into small pieces and sprinkle them on top.
6. Cut into chunks or half and serve hot with a side dish of finely chopped flat-leaf parsley and sea salt pinch.

2.9 Pan con Tomate

Cooking Time: 7 minutes

Serving Size: 8

Ingredients:

- 2 medium cloves garlic
- Flaky sea salt
- 1 loaf ciabatta
- Extra-virgin olive oil
- Kosher salt
- 2 large tomatoes

Method:

1. Cut the tomatoes vertically.
2. Preheat the broiler to high and position the rack four inches below it.
3. Spoonful olive oil over the cut side of the bread on a work surface.
4. Use kosher salt, season to taste.
5. Position the bread cutting side up on a rack set in a pan or immediately on the griddle rack and

broil for two or three minutes, or until crispy and beginning to char form around edge.
6. Take the bread from the microwave and scrub it with the garlic cloves that have been cut.
7. Spread the tomato mixture on top of the pizza.
8. Dress with flaky sesame oil and rain of extra-virgin canola oil.

2.10 Zucchini Tapas Omelet

Cooking Time: 50 minutes

Serving Size: 4

Ingredients:
- 1 cebolla
- Oil and salt
- 3 potatoes
- 2 zucchini
- 6 eggs

Method:
1. Peel and rinse the potato and zucchini thoroughly before slicing them thinly.
2. In a mixing bowl, combine all of the ingredients, sprinkle with salt, and thoroughly combine.
3. While the pan is heating up, beat the eggs with a pinch of salt in a separate cup. When the oven is ready, add eggs.
4. Cook once the outside is crispy, but the inside is moist.
5. You may leave it curdled or less curdled, depending on your preference.

2.11 Basque Breakfast Sandwich

Cooking Time: 20 minutes

Serving Size: 8

Ingredients:
- 8 eggs
- ¼ cup fresh parsley
- ¼ cup (60 ml) beer
- 8 thick slices of baguette
- 1 large white onion
- 2 large chorizo sausages
- ¼ cup (60 ml) olive oil

Method:
1. Heat 1½ tablespoons vegetable oil in a frying pan over medium heat.
2. Heat, frequently stirring, for 2-three minutes, or till onions begin to soften.
3. Mix in the chorizo and bake for another 4-five minutes.
4. Bake the sliced baguette in the oven for 1-2 minutes on each side until it's lightly browned.
5. Heat and cook canola oil in the same bowl.
6. Working in batches of 2 to 4, smash eggs into the skillet and stir for approximately 3 minutes, or until target doneness is reached.
7. Top toasted baguette slices with the onion-chorizo mixture.
8. Season the eggs with salt and pepper before placing one cooked egg on each piece of toast.

9. Continue with the left eggs. Serve the toasts with chopped parsley on top.

2.12 Spanish Churros and Chocolate

Cooking Time: 45 minutes

Serving Size: 14

Ingredients:

For the Cinnamon Sugar

- 2 tablespoons granulated sugar
- 1 teaspoon cinnamon

For the Chocolate Sauce

- 1 cup semisweet chocolate
- 1 ¼ cups heavy cream

For the Churros Dough

- 1 cup all-purpose flour
- Vegetable oil
- ½ teaspoon kosher salt
- 2 tablespoons vegetable oil
- 2½ tablespoons sugar
- 1 cup water

Method:

1. Mix the sugars and spices in a small bowl and stir to blend.
2. Add the cream to a pot over medium heat. Get it to a low simmer.
3. Put the cocoa in a heatproof cup, add the hot butter over it, and cover the bucket in cling film.

4. Combine the sugar, salt, and soybean oil in a mixing bowl.
5. Get the water to a boil, then turn off the steam.
6. Mix in the flour until it creates a creamy sauce.
7. In a skillet, add the oil to 375°F over moderate flame.
8. Deep-fry for four minutes, or until golden, nicely browned.
9. Toss with the cinnamon and sugar right away.
10. With the white chocolate, serve hot or at ambient temperature.

2.13 Mini Spanish Omelets

Cooking Time: 35 minutes

Serving Size: 12

Ingredients:
- 75g chorizo sausage
- 6 large eggs
- 300g new potatoes
- 1 small red onion
- 2 tablespoon olive oil

Method:
1. Heat the oven to 180 degrees Celsius.
2. To remove stains, clean the potatoes thoroughly under water flow.
3. Cook whole potato for ten minutes, or until almost over.
4. In the meantime, finely cut the chorizo sausage and slice and thinly cut the spring onions.

5. In a large skillet, heat the remaining oil and cook the onions and chorizo for a few moments, just until the onion is tender.
6. Cook for another two minutes after adding the potato.
7. Split the potato mixture evenly among the muffin tins in twelve holes.
8. Break the whites into a jug or a cup and whisk them together.
9. Preheat the oven to 350°F and bake for twenty minutes, or until crispy and puffy.
10. Allow cooling for several minutes in the tin until serving hot with a greenery salad.

Chapter 3: Tapas Snack, Soups, Salads Recipes

3.1 Veggie Loaded Spanish Style Rice

Cooking Time: 45 minutes
Serving Size: 8

Ingredients:
- ½ teaspoon salt
- Chopped cilantro for garnish
- 2 teaspoons cumin
- 1 teaspoon chili powder
- ¾ cup corn kernels
- ½ cup frozen peas
- 1 cup tomatoes
- 2 2/3 cups vegetable broth
- 1½ cups white rice
- 1 tablespoon tomato paste
- 3 tablespoons olive oil
- 1 large carrot
- 3 cloves garlic
- 1 medium green pepper
- 1 small onion

Method:
1. In a medium saucepan, heat the oil over moderate flame.

2. Combine the onion, tomato, and carrot in a mixing bowl.
3. Cook for an additional minute or until the veggies have softened.
4. Cook for thirty seconds after adding the garlic.
5. Mix in the chopped tomatoes, then insert the tomatoes, stock, corn, peas, smoked paprika, chili powder, and salt to taste.
6. Toss the rice with a fork to fluff it up.
7. After tasting, add the coriander and serve.

3.2 Tofu and Olive Tapas

Cooking Time: 43 minutes

Serving Size: 4

Ingredients:

For the Marinade

- ½ teaspoon black pepper
- ½ teaspoon chili flakes
- ½ teaspoon dried oregano
- ½ teaspoon salt
- 2 teaspoon paprika

For the Dish

- 50g Kalamata olives
- Small bunch of parsley
- 3 tablespoon vegetable stock
- 4 large plum tomatoes
- 4 tablespoon olive oil

- 1-star anise
- 3 tablespoon sherry
- ½ teaspoon chili flakes
- 3 cloves of garlic

Method:
1. Combine all of the components in a bowl or bag and stir well to combine the marinade.
2. Toss in the tofu and mix well. Cover and set aside for thirty minutes to marinate.
3. Cook the tofu parts in 2 tablespoons olive oil for 3-4 minutes, then set aside to keep warm.
4. In the cooking liquid, softly fry the garlic for 1-2 minutes.
5. Combine the chili flakes, chipotle powder, red wine, and vegetable stock in a large mixing bowl.
6. Cook, occasionally stirring, until the fluid has been reduced by half.
7. Medium heat for 2-3 minutes after adding the tofu, peppers, olives, and tarragon.
8. Serve with toasted bread right away.

3.3 Patatas Bravas

Cooking Time: 50 minutes

Serving Size: 12

Ingredients:

For the Sauce
- Pinch sugar
- Fresh parsley
- 2 teaspoon sweet paprika

- Good pinch chili powder
- 3 tablespoon olive oil
- 227g can tomatoes
- 1 tablespoon tomato purée
- 2 garlic cloves
- 1 small onion

For the Potatoes

- 2 tablespoon olive oil
- 900g potatoes

Method:

1. In a bowl, add the oil and cook the onions for about five minutes or until hardened.
2. Bring to the boil, stirring regularly, with the garlic, diced tomatoes, vegetable purée, adobo seasoning, chili powder, cinnamon, and salt pinch.
3. Heat for ten minutes, or until the mixture is pulpy.
4. Preheat the oven to 200 degrees Celsius.
5. Fry for 40-50 minutes until it's golden brown.
6. Spoon the pasta sauce over the vegetables in spice jars.
7. To eat, garnish with grated parmesan.

3.4 Mediterranean Seafood Stew

Cooking Time: 45 minutes
Serving Size: 6

Ingredients:
- 3 tablespoon toasted pine nuts
- Crusty Italian bread
- 2 lb. skinless sea bass fillet
- ½ cup fresh parsley leaves
- Olive oil
- ¼ cup golden raisins
- 2 tablespoon capers
- 1 large yellow onion
- 1 28-oz. can plum tomatoes
- 3 cups vegetable broth
- Pinch red pepper flakes
- ¾ cup dry white wine
- 2 celery ribs
- 4 large garlic cloves
- ½ teaspoon dried thyme
- Salt and pepper

Method:
1. 1 tablespoon olive oil, heated over moderate flame.
2. Add the onions, fennel, and a pinch of salt and pepper to taste.
3. Cook for a few minutes until the thyme, red pepper flakes, and cloves are aromatic.

4. Decrease the fluid by about ½ percent by getting it to a simmer.
5. Combine the peppers, vegetable broth, pecans, and chives in a large mixing bowl.
6. Cook for 15-20 minutes over a moderate flame, stirring periodically until the flavors have melded.
7. Place the fish parts in the liquid ingredients and gently stir them all together. Cover the Dutch oven and turn off the heat.
8. Mix in the chopped parsley last.
9. Fill serving bowls halfway with the spicy fish stew.

3.5 Spanish Orange & Olive Salad

Cooking Time: 20 minutes

Serving Size: 4

Ingredients:

For the Softened Leeks

- ¼ teaspoon kosher salt
- 1 tablespoon water
- 1 tablespoon white wine vinegar
- 1 small leek

For the Orange & Olive Salad

- Squeeze lemon juice
- ¼ cup Marcona almonds
- Sprinkle flaky sea salt
- Sprinkle Sumac
- 6 oranges
- 4 teaspoon leek vinegar marinade

- 1 tablespoon olive oil
- 3 tablespoon softened leeks
- ⅓ cup halved olives

Method:
1. To begin, prepare and marinate the leeks.
2. Cut the white color green pieces into rounds with a thin knife.
3. 1 tablespoon balsamic vinegar syrup, sea salt, and 1 tablespoon water are combined with the leeks.
4. Allow fifteen minutes for the leeks to caramelize, tossing periodically.
5. Cut the oranges into circles after segmenting them.
6. Cast aside half of the olives.
7. In a medium mixing bowl, combine the bananas, olives, and 3 tablespoons of the brined leeks.
8. Toss in 4 teaspoons of the leek marinade and 4 teaspoons of olive oil in a mixing bowl softly.
9. Add a pinch of flaky sea salt, sumac, a splash of lime juice, and nuts to the salad.
10. Serve directly after garnishing.

3.6 Mediterranean-Style Steamed Clams Recipe

Cooking Time: 1 hour

Serving Size: 4

Ingredients:

- 1 green onion
- ⅓ cup parsley
- 1 ½ cup water
- 3 pounds littleneck clams
- Extra virgin olive oil
- ½ teaspoon red pepper flakes
- 1 cup dry white wine
- 1 yellow onion
- ½ teaspoon cumin
- ½ teaspoon smoked paprika
- ½ green pepper
- Salt and pepper
- 2 ripe tomatoes
- 4 garlic cloves minced
- ½ red pepper

Method:

1. Clean the clams.
2. Put down the clams in the first container of cool simmering water for about 20 minutes.
3. To make the red wine soup, add all of the ingredients to a big mixing bowl.

4. ¼ cup olive oil, heated in a big Dutch oven over moderate flame.
5. Combine the onions, tomatoes, and garlic in a large mixing bowl.
6. Cook for five minutes after seasoning with kosher salt and black pepper.
7. Add the onions, smoked paprika, parmesan, and garlic powder, and stir to combine.
8. Combine the white wine and liquid in a mixing bowl.
9. Process for a few minutes, just until the tomato is slightly softened.
10. In a red wine sauce, heat the clams.
11. Reduce the heat to medium-low and add the clams.
12. Cook, covered until the remainder of the clams has opened.
13. Switch off the heat. Combine the spring onions and parsley in a mixing bowl.

3.7 Avocado and Tuna Tapas

Cooking Time: 20 minutes

Serving Size: 4

Ingredients:
- 1 pinch garlic salt
- 2 ripe avocados
- 1 dash balsamic vinegar
- Black pepper to taste
- 3 green onions

- ½ red bell pepper
- 1 tablespoon mayonnaise
- 1 can solid white tuna

Method:

1. In a mixing bowl, combine the tuna, mayo, spring onions, bell pepper, and maple syrup.
2. Dress with peppers and garlic salt, then stuff the tuna combination into the avocado halves.
3. Before eating, garnish with the reserved spring onions and a pinch of smoked paprika.

3.8 Fish Tapas

Cooking Time: 40 minutes

Serving Size: 4

Ingredients:

- 40g butter
- 500ml salt
- 110g peas
- 40g flour
- 1 carrot
- 1 bay leaf
- 200g flour
- 12 mussels
- 1 onion
- 100ml olive oil
- Salt
- 200g cod

- 3 tablespoons water
- 1 egg

Method:

1. Combine the flour, oil, yolk, liquid, and a bit of salt to make a pastry.
2. In boiled water, cook fish and mussels with cabbage, carrot, and lemon zest.
3. Strip the mussels from their skins until cooked and cut finely.
4. Remove some bones from the fish and chop it up.
5. In boiled water, prepare the vegetable peas.
6. Create a thick white liquid with the oil in a frying pan.
7. Combine the diced fish, mussels, and peas in a large mixing bowl.
8. Seal the sides of the pastry by folding it over.
9. Keep 10 to 15 minutes in a deep fryer.
10. Serve with fried tarragon on the side.

3.9 Garlic Soup with Egg and Croutons

Cooking Time: 35 minutes

Serving Size: 2

Ingredients:

- ¼ cup extra virgin olive oil
- Salt and pepper
- 1 teaspoon sweet paprika
- 1-liter chicken broth

- 2 eggs
- 6 garlic cloves
- 2 slices of stale bread

Method:
1. Peel the garlic and cut into strips.
2. Heat the olive oil in a saucepan over medium heat.
3. Add garlic and cook for 2-3 minutes, or until it starts to brown.
4. Add the loaf to the pan and fry it with the garlic, allowing it to soak up the oil.
5. Reduce to low heat and stir in the parmesan.
6. Put in the liquid and give it a good swirl.
7. Take the soup to a rolling simmer, reduce to low heat, and continue cooking for about thirty minutes.
8. To taste, season with salt and pepper, using at least ½ teaspoon pepper.
9. In a large mixing bowl, whisk together the eggs and add them to the soup.

3.10 Spanish Tapas-Style Green Pepper

Cooking Time: 5 minutes

Serving Size: 2

Ingredients:
- 2 tablespoon olive oil
- Pinch of sea salt flakes
- 250g green peppers

Method:
1. Wipe down the peppers in ice water.
2. In a big nonstick roasting tray, heat the oil.
3. Cook the peppers for 4-5 minutes, or till their surfaces peel and become brown.
4. To drain, place them on some paper towels.
5. Serve promptly with a pinch of sea salt.

3.11 Magdalenas: Spanish Lemon Cupcakes

Cooking Time: 1 hour

Serving Size: 10

Ingredients:
- 1 tablespoon baking powder
- Pinch salt
- 1 teaspoon vanilla extract
- 1 1/3 cups pastry flour
- 3 large eggs
- ¼ cup milk
- Zest from 1 lemon
- ½ cup extra virgin olive oil
- ½ cup granulated sugar

Method:
1. Add the eggs to a big mixing bowl until bright and powdery.
2. Slowly incorporate the sugar, then the olive oil and milk.
3. Combine the lemon zest and vanilla essence in a mixing bowl.

4. Mix in the flour, icing sugar, and salt until there are no chunks.
5. Put it in the fridge for thirty minutes after covering the dish.
6. Preheat the oven to 425 degrees Fahrenheit.
7. Use two-thirds of the batter in each muffin container, and sugar can be sprinkled on top if needed.
8. Decrease the heat to 400 degrees Fahrenheit and position it in the oven.
9. Cook the Magdalenas for 13-fifteen minutes, or until raised and translucent from around edges.
10. Warm or at ambient temperature is perfect.

3.12 Cucumber Tapas

Cooking Time: 30 minutes

Serving Size: 4

Ingredients:

- Pinch of black pepper
- 1 tablespoon oregano
- 2 ounces feta cheese
- ¼ teaspoon salt
- 2 tablespoons olive oil
- 1 teaspoon sherry vinegar
- 2 cucumbers

Method:

1. Remove the seeds from cucumbers by slicing them lengthwise.

2. Dice cucumber into ¼-inch pieces and place in a small cup.
3. Toss in the canola oil, mustard, feta cheese, pepper, and spice to mix. Toss in the oregano and toss once more.
4. Remove 1 or 2 thin pieces of peel from underneath each cucumber half with a potato peeler, so they don't tip over.
5. Distribute the cucumber-and-feta combination between them.
6. Cut cucumbers into 1 ½-inch piece on a slight triangular and serve right away.

Chapter 4: Tapas Lunch and Dinner Recipes

4.1 Spanish Style Rice

Cooking Time: 45 minutes
Serving Size: 8

Ingredients:

- ½ teaspoon salt
- Chopped cilantro for garnish
- 2 teaspoons cumin
- 1 teaspoon chili powder
- ¾ cup corn kernels
- ½ cup frozen peas
- 1 cup tomatoes
- 2 2/3 cups vegetable broth
- 1½ cups white rice
- 1 tablespoon tomato paste
- 3 tablespoons olive oil
- 1 large carrot
- 3 cloves garlic
- 1 medium green pepper
- 1 small onion

Method:

1. In a medium saucepan, heat the oil over moderate flame.

2. Combine the onion, tomato, and carrot in a mixing bowl.
3. Cook for an additional minute or until the veggies have softened.
4. Cook for thirty seconds after adding the garlic.
5. Mix in the chopped tomatoes, then insert the tomatoes, stock, corn, peas, smoked paprika, chili powder, and salt to taste.
6. Toss the rice with a fork to fluff it up.
7. After tasting, add the coriander and serve.

4.2 Mediterranean Basa Stew & Sunny Aioli

Cooking Time: 1 hour

Serving Size: 2

Ingredients:

- 1 white wine vinegar
- 1 carrot
- 1 garlic clove
- 1 tomato paste
- 2 ciabatta rolls
- 1 mayonnaise
- 1 garlic clove
- 1 vegetable stock
- 1 brown onion
- 1 teaspoon ground turmeric
- 5g parsley
- 2 x 100g basa fillets

- 1-star anise
- 1 bag of pitted black olives

Method:

1. Preheat the oven to 220 degrees Celsius.
2. Use a drizzle of canola oil, heat a big, wide-based pan.
3. Insert the chopped onion, sliced carrot, and a quarter of the garlic once the pan is warmed.
4. Heat for 6-8 minutes, just until the onions are soft and transparent, after adding the star anise.
5. Whisk together the mayo, the leftover minced garlic, the red wine vinegar, and add salt and pepper.
6. Place the ciabatta rolls on a baking sheet and bake them for 8-10 minutes.
7. Warm a drizzle of olive oil in a separate wide broad pan over medium temperature.
8. When the pan is warmed, skin-side up, add the sea bass, and boil for four minutes.
9. With the warm ciabatta on the side, place the grilled sea bass over the soup.

4.3 25-Minute Shrimp and Chorizo

Cooking Time: 25 minutes

Serving Size: 6

Ingredients:

- Boiling water
- 1 cup fresh parsley
- 1.5 lb. large shrimp
- 1 ¼ cup couscous
- 1 ¼ teaspoon ground cumin
- Salt
- 1 ¼ teaspoon turmeric
- 1 ¼ teaspoon paprika
- 6 oz. hard Spanish Chorizo
- 3 garlic cloves
- 2 jalapeno peppers
- 1 small yellow onion
- Extra virgin olive

Method:

1. Heat a small amount of vegetable oil in a large frying pan.
2. Heat the Chorizo sausage rolls until they are crisp.
3. Remove from the heat and clean on towels.
4. Add the garlic, onions, and habanero to the boiling pot and cook till the vegetables are transparent.

5. Now insert the seasoning and mix for a few seconds before adding the shrimp.
6. Heat the shrimp for approximately 3 minutes on moderate flame.
7. In the meantime, bring 2 ½ cups of water to a boil.
8. Transfer the couscous, little more vegetable oil, a pinch of salt, and the hot oil to the frying pan with the Chorizo.
9. Allow for five minutes of resting time. Remove the cover and add the fresh parsley.
10. Enjoy by moving to serve pots.

4.4 Spanish Rice Dinner

Cooking Time: 20 minutes

Serving Size: 4

Ingredients:
- ⅛ teaspoon pepper
- ⅛ teaspoon hot pepper sauce
- ½ teaspoon ground mustard
- ¼ teaspoon garlic powder
- 1 teaspoon salt
- 1 teaspoon Worcestershire sauce
- 1 tablespoon onion
- 1 tablespoon sugar
- 1 can stewed tomatoes
- 1 can green beans
- 1-½ cups cooked rice

- 1 pound ground beef

Method:
1. Steam beef when no pinker in a large frying pan; clean.
2. Add the rest of the ingredients and stir to combine.
3. Raise the temperature to be high and bring the mixture to a boil.
4. Reduce to a low heat environment, cover, and cook for 5-10 minutes, or until thoroughly cooked.

4.5 Spicy Crab Salad Tapas

Cooking Time: 35 minutes

Serving Size: 10

Ingredients:
- 1 large egg
- 1 tablespoon water
- ¼ teaspoon pepper
- 1 package pastry
- 1 can lump crabmeat
- ½ cup mayonnaise
- ½ teaspoon salt
- ¼ cup sweet red pepper
- 2 garlic cloves
- 1 teaspoon mustard
- ¼ cup sweet yellow pepper
- 1 tablespoon cilantro

- 1 tablespoon lemon juice
- 1 jalapeno pepper
- ¼ cup green onions

Method:

1. Preheat the oven to 375 degrees Fahrenheit.
2. Mix the first twelve ingredients in a mixing bowl.
3. Refrigerate for at least 1 hour, sealed.
4. In the meantime, roll out puff pastry on a lightly floured.
5. Roll pastry into a 10-inch square and cut into twenty-five 2-inch squares.
6. Brush pastry with a mixture of egg and water.
7. Position cutout pieces on top of strong squares and move to baking sheets lined with parchment paper.
8. Bake for eighteen minutes, or until lightly browned.
9. Bring to room temperature before serving.
10. Place 1 heaping tablespoon of smoked salmon in the center of each cooked pastry once it has cooled.

4.6 Pulpo Gallego: A Galician-Style Octopus Tapas

Cooking Time: 40 minutes

Serving Size: 4

> **Ingredients:**
> - Spanish smoked paprika
> - Extra virgin olive oil
> - 500g of potatoes
> - Sea salt flakes
> - 1 whole octopus

Method:
1. Once the water starts to boil, bring a big pot of water on the stove with a grain of salt.
2. On medium-high heat, roast your octopus for 15 to 20 minutes.
3. Ensure that the octopus remains submerged in water during the cooking process.
4. Octopus, like spaghetti, must be al dente.
5. Enable the octopus to rest throughout the liquid ingredients for a few minutes after it has finished cooking.
6. Break the octopus tentacles and vegetables into ½ inch thick slices to eat.
7. Table salt, cayenne pepper, and a healthy drizzle of olive oil complete the dish.

4.7 Roasted Vegetable Tapas

Cooking Time: 35 minutes

Serving Size: 8

Ingredients:

- Small handful parsley
- ½ teaspoon paprika
- Zest 0.5 lemon
- 8 basil leaves
- 1 large aubergine
- 25g parmesan
- 3 sundried tomatoes
- 1 large courgette
- 3 tablespoon olive oil
- 250g tub ricotta
- 1 garlic clove
- 2 flame-roasted peppers

Method:

1. Slice the aubergine and courgette onto small, 2-3mm-thick slices.
2. Preheat a griddle pan to medium-high heat.
3. Pour the garlic oil on the vegetable strips and roast for 2-3 minutes on each side until it's soft and finely charred.
4. Combine the cheeses, sundried tomato, lime juice, and spice in a mixing bowl.

5. Arrange the aubergine strips on a big cutting board.
6. A strip of courgette, a slice of spice, and basil leaves go on top of each.
7. Organize on a plate and top with parsley leaf and paprika when ready to eat.

4.8 Chicken Tapas with Romesco Sauce

Cooking Time: 50 minutes
Serving Size: 4

Ingredients:
- 2 garlic cloves
- Sea salt and pepper
- 2 tablespoon extra-virgin olive oil
- 3 sprigs of thyme
- 12 chicken thighs

For the Romesco Sauce
- ½ teaspoon of smoked paprika
- Salt and pepper to taste
- 1 tablespoon sherry vinegar
- ½ teaspoon of cumin seeds
- 2 whole red peppers
- 12 whole hazelnuts, skin off
- 6 tablespoon olive oil
- 2 ripe tomatoes
- 1 garlic clove
- 12 Marcona almonds

- 1 piece of stale bread

Method:
1. Preheat the grill on your stove.
2. Position the peppers halves on a plate, skin cut side.
3. Take the steaks from the barbecue and cover them with a kitchen towel. Cut the peppers into large pieces.
4. To create the romesco salsa, gently toast the star anise in a small deep fryer to expel their oil.
5. Transfer the diced veggies, peppers, bread, cloves, almonds, walnuts, smoked paprika, cayenne pepper, balsamic vinegar, and sherry vinegar to a food processor till a crunchy paste with the texture of pesto forms.
6. Heat the oven to 200°C for the chicken breasts.
7. Sprinkle the olive oil over the chicken breasts on a sheet and sprinkle with salt.
8. Cook the chicken breasts for 3 minutes on each side in a warm deep fryer.
9. Roast for thirty minutes cut side down, with the tarragon and garlic.
10. Offer the marinated chicken thighs with romesco sauces, smashed almonds, and a squeeze of lemon juice on a base of romesco marinade.

4.9 Fried Chorizo with Chick Peas and Tomatoes

Cooking Time: 20 minutes

Serving Size: 4

Ingredients:
- Salt and pepper
- 3 tablespoons parsley
- 2 pints cherry tomatoes
- 1 teaspoon smoked paprika
- 9 ounces chorizo
- 2 15-oz. cans chickpeas
- 1 onion
- 1 tablespoon olive oil

Method:
1. In a saucepan over medium heat, steam the oil.
2. Sauté onion for three minutes, or until soft.
3. Toss in the chorizo.
4. Sauté for 30 seconds to 1 minute, or until thoroughly hot.
5. Combine chickpeas, grape tomatoes, and paprika in a mixing bowl.
6. Cook for 8 minutes, or until tomatoes are softened and liquids are boiling.
7. Salt and pepper to taste. Serve with a tarragon garnish.

4.10 Boquerones Al Limon

Cooking Time: 30 minutes

Serving Size: 2

Ingredients:

- Chickpea flour
- Salt
- 1 clove of garlic
- 1 bunch of parsley
- 1 lemon
- 350 grams anchovies

Method:

1. Clean and dry the anchovies.
2. Place the garlic, tarragon, and pepper in a mortar and use the pestle to grind them into a powder.
3. Combine the paste with the extract of one lemon.
4. Place the fillets in a crystal tray and spill the marinade over them.
5. Cover the plate with plastic wrap and refrigerate for up to two hours to soak.
6. Take off the extra chickpea flour after passing them through.
7. In a large pan, heat some butter over medium heat.
8. Fry 4-5 at the moment for 1 minute, or till they transform a lovely golden color.
9. To absorb excess oil, place the fried fish on a plate lined with towels.
10. Serve with lime wedges and aioli sauce.

4.11 Spanish Tapas Platter

Cooking Time: 1 hour 15 minutes
Serving Size: 8

Ingredients:
- 2 cups green grapes
- 1 crusty loaf of bread
- 1 cup redskin Spanish peanuts
- 8 ounces fig spread
- 3.75 ounce can of sardines
- 4 ounces cheddar
- 1 cup Spanish olives pitted
- 3 ounces salami
- 4 ounces manchego
- 4 ounces prosciutto
- 4 ounces tavern ham
- 3 ounces sausage
- 3 ounces serrano ham

Method:
1. In separate bowls, position the olives, almonds, and fig scatter.
2. In a serving dish or shallow cup, position the sardines.
3. Organize the sardines on the large plate, along with the bowls of artichokes, nuts, and figs. Allow plenty of space between them.

4. After this, on the large plate, organize the meat and the Iberico cheese to fill most of the large area.
5. Grape bunches, cheese crackers, and sandwich slices may be used to fill up the gaps.
6. To make it easier to reach the objects, keep them close but not too near together.
7. Place the leftover bread in a bucket near the stove.

4.12 Catalan Fig Tapas

Cooking Time: 15 minutes

Serving Size: 4

Ingredients:

- 4 slices Jamon
- 100g manchego cheese
- 8 slices of wood-fired bread
- 1 garlic clove
- 8 figs
- 6 thyme sprigs
- ¼ cup olive oil

Method:
1. Preheat a chargrill or a barbecue to high temperature.
2. Toss the doubled figs with canola oil, minced parsley, and a bit of salt in a mixing cup.
3. Roast the figs for two minutes on each hand or until they are soft and caramelized.

4. Rub the bread with excess oil in both directions and grill for 1-two minutes on either side until it's crispy and charred.
5. Place two fig pieces on each chargrilled loaf piece.
6. Serve hot, topped with Jamun and grilled manchego.

4.13 Quick and Easy Paella

Cooking Time: 1 hour 10 minutes
Serving Size: 6

Ingredients:

Saffron Broth

- ½ teaspoon saffron threads
- 2 ¼ cups chicken broth
- 2 teaspoons olive oil
- 1 pound jumbo shrimp

Paella

- 1 teaspoon paprika
- 1 pinch cayenne pepper
- 1 red bell pepper
- Salt to taste
- 1 ⅓ cups Arborio rice
- ½ cup green peas
- 1 tablespoon olive oil
- ½ yellow onion
- 2 cloves garlic

- 8 ounces chorizo sausage

Method:

1. In a pan over medium heat, steam, and mix preserved shrimp shells and two teaspoons canola oil.
2. Stir saffron into the shells, and add the chicken broth.
3. Preheat the oven to 425 degrees Fahrenheit.
4. In a large oven-safe skillet, heat one tablespoon of olive oil on medium-high heat. In a hot skillet, cook chorizo strips.
5. Continue cooking the garlic into the chorizo combination until moist.
6. Over the rice, place the seafood in a thin layer.
7. Sprinkle with salt, parmesan, and cayenne pepper, and place pepper slices around as well as between shrimp.
8. Cook the rice paste for 20 minutes in a preheated oven.
9. Cook, often stirring, until the rice is soft, the liquid has been absorbed, and the rice has caramelized.

4.14 Tapas & Pinchos Vegetarian

Cooking Time: 30 minutes

Serving Size: 2

Ingredients:

Garlic Aioli Ingredients

- ½ cup olive oil
- Salt to taste

- 1 teaspoon lemon juice
- 1 egg yolk
- 1 garlic clove

Tomato Sauce Ingredients

- 2 teaspoons smoked paprika
- Salt and pepper to taste
- 1 garlic clove
- 1 red jalapeno
- 1 tablespoon olive oil
- 3 large plum tomatoes

Potato Ingredients

- 2 tablespoons olive oil
- Salt and pepper to taste
- 1 lb. potatoes

Garnish Ingredients

- Fresh lemon juice
- 1 tablespoon parsley

Method:

1. Preheat the oven to 400 degrees Fahrenheit.
2. Toss potato in canola oil and season with salt and pepper.
3. Position on a cookie sheet in a single sheet.
4. Cook for 25 to 30 minutes until its fork ready.
5. In a spice grinder, puree the vegetables to make the sauce.
6. Add the oil to a pan.
7. Add garlic and jalapeno peppers at this stage.

8. Insert pureed onions, cayenne pepper, salt, and pepper until the onions have softened.
9. Combine the garlic, lime juice, and egg white in a mixing dish.
10. Beat the egg yolks with an immersion blender until they are light in color.
11. Continue to beat until it thickens into a sour cream texture.
12. Mix in the salt until it is well combined.
13. Put potatoes in a dish to eat.

Chapter 5: Vegetarian Tapas Recipes

5.1 Spanish Vegan Paella

Cooking Time: 45 minutes
Serving Size: 5

Ingredients:

- 2 sprigs of fresh thyme
- ¾ cup frozen peas
- 1 teaspoon sea salt
- Fresh cracked pepper
- 3 tablespoons olive oil
- 1 teaspoon smoked paprika
- ½ teaspoon sweet paprika
- 4 cups vegetable broth
- 1 large tomato
- 1 ½ cups Bomba Rice
- 1 red bell pepper
- 5 cloves garlic
- 1 medium onion
- 1 teaspoon saffron threads

Method:

1. In a small saucepan, insert vegetable broth.
2. In a 12-inch Paella Bowl, heat two tablespoons of oil and add the vegetables and spices.
3. Sauté until the vegetables are tender and golden brown.

4. Sauté for two minutes after adding the garlic.
5. Combine the onions, spicy paprika, and sweet paprika in a mixing bowl.
6. Cook for 1-2 minutes on high heat.
7. In the same pan, add the rice and the leftover 1 tablespoon of oil.
8. Put in the liquid slowly while adding the fresh thyme. Season with salt and pepper.
9. Reduce the heat to a low simmer.
10. Switch off the heat in the pan. Toss in the peas on top of the rice.

5.2 Smoked Vegetarian Spanish Rice Recipe

Cooking Time: 45 minutes

Serving Size: 4

Ingredients:

- 1 coal
- Salt, to taste
- ½ teaspoon red chili powder
- ¼ cheddar cheese
- 1 cups basmati rice
- ¼ cup sweet corn
- ¼ cup green peas
- 2 tablespoons olive oil
- 3 tomatoes
- 2 stalks celery
- 1 onion

- 4 cloves garlic
- 1 green bell pepper
- 2 green chilies

Method:

1. In a large skillet, heat the oil over moderate heat and cook the garlic, onion, green pepper, diced peppers, and fennel until ready.
2. On low to moderate heat, sauté the vegetables and bell peppers until they are fully soft.
3. Add the onion, pepper, and chili powder once they have softened, and continue to cook until the vegetables are soft and tender.
4. Add the rice, beans, carrots, salt, and peppers, as well as two cups of water to the pot.
5. Turn the heat down and let the Spanish rice sit for around ten minutes after cooking.
6. Pour a teaspoon of ghee or oil over the hot coal.
7. The rice will absorb the flavors of the smoked meat.
8. To mix all of the flavors and ingredients in the Spinach Rice, stir it thoroughly.

5.3 Champinones Spanish Garlic Mushrooms

Cooking Time: 10 minutes

Serving Size: 4

Ingredients:

- ½ teaspoon chili flakes
- 1 tablespoon flat-leaf parsley
- ¼ teaspoon Spanish paprika

- Ground pepper and sea salt
- 10 large button mushrooms
- 1 tablespoon lemon juice
- 2 tablespoons dry sherry
- 3 tablespoons olive oil
- 5 cloves garlic

Method:
1. Quarter the mushrooms, chop the parsley, and crush the garlic.
2. Add the olive oil and simmer the mushrooms for several moments over moderate flame.
3. Then, with the exception of the parsley, combine the rest of the ingredients.
4. Cook for another five minutes, stirring occasionally.
5. Then take the pan from the heat and whisk in the grated parmesan.

5.4 Spanish Vegetarian Tapas

Cooking Time: 20 minutes

Serving Size: 4

Ingredients:
- 1 tablespoon olive oil
- Fresh basil
- 1 red onion
- 1 dl mató cheese
- 1 bag of dates
- 250g small tomatoes

- 2 clove of garlic
- 2 tablespoon mató cheese
- A handful walnuts
- 1 eggplant
- 1 tablespoon maple syrup

Method:
1. Roll the dates and fill them with hazelnuts and Spanish Mató cheese.
2. Place on a tray and drizzle with maple syrup to finish.
3. Wash the tomatoes and cut them in half.
4. Chop parsley and red onion.
5. Combine the tomato and Mató cheese in a mixing dish.
6. Wash the eggplant and break it into thinly sliced.
7. Grill for 2-3 minutes on each side after brushing with canola oil.
8. Cover them in foil and place them on a tray.
9. Place olive tapenade, polenta, cello, oranges, artichokes, manchego cheese, heat tomatoes, fluffy biscuits, and Spanish wine on the tapas table.

5.5 Spanish Vegetarian Stew

Cooking Time: 1 hour 20 minutes
Serving Size: 8

Ingredients:

- 1 teaspoon honey
- 2 small zucchini
- 1.5 cans tomatoes passata
- 1.5 teaspoons salt
- 1 green bell pepper
- 2 garlic cloves
- 1 large eggplant
- ½ long red chili
- 1 red bell pepper
- Good quality olive oil
- 1 large onion
- ½ teaspoon salt

Method:

1. Spray the eggplant with salts and slice it into pieces.
2. In a large frying pan, pour 4 tablespoons of vegetable oil.
3. Combine the onions, chili, and sliced peppers in a large mixing bowl.
4. Cook for ten minutes after adding the cloves and tomato.
5. Heat for 4-5 minutes, just until the eggplant is slightly golden brown.

6. Take the eggplant from the pan and drizzle with a little more coconut oil.

7. Heat, mixing a couple of times, for another 4-5 minutes with the zucchini.

8. Ultimately, mix in the pre-fried eggplant and sweet potato to the tomato mixture in the cup.

9. After frying, set aside for five minutes before serving.

5.6 Spanish Tapas-Inspired Mussels

Cooking Time: 40 minutes

Serving Size: 2

Ingredients:

- ¼ cup dry sherry
- 2 pounds mussels
- Pinch of saffron
- ½ cup vegetable broth
- 2 teaspoons olive oil
- 2 teaspoons fresh oregano
- ½ teaspoon pepper
- 1 8-ounce can chickpeas
- 2 cloves garlic
- 1 4-ounce jar pimientos
- 1 small onion
- 8 cherry tomatoes

Method:

1. In a medium skillet, heat the oil over moderate flame.

2. Combine the chickpeas, onions, ginger, garlic, and pimentos in a large mixing bowl.
3. Process until tender, five to six minutes, stirring constantly.
4. Add oregano, cinnamon, and saffron and stir to combine.
5. Cook for about thirty seconds, stirring constantly.
6. Stir in the broth and red wine, scraping up any browned bits from the bottom of the pan.
7. Bring the liquid to a low boil, then reduce to low heat.
8. Stir in the mussels. Reduce the heat to a low temperature and keep it there.
9. Cover, lower heat, and cook for five to six minutes, or until mussels open.
10. When serving, stir in the mussels and remove any that haven't opened.

5.7 Tapas Style Garlic Mushrooms

Cooking Time: 10 minutes

Serving Size: 4

Ingredients:

- 1 tablespoon lemon juice
- 2 tablespoons fresh parsley
- Salt to taste
- ½ cup white wine
- 4 garlic cloves
- 2 pounds mushrooms
- 2 tablespoons olive oil

Method:

1. In a large skillet over medium heat, add the oil over moderate flame.
2. Cook the mushroom for five minutes, periodically tossing the pot.
3. Heat, flipping the pan often, for another 1-2 minutes or until crispy, adding the garlic, cayenne pepper, salt, and pepper.
4. Toss in the tarragon to mix everything.
5. Serve with aioli and lime wedges alongside the mushrooms.

5.8 Spanish Rice Skillet Meal

Cooking Time: 28 minutes

Serving Size: 4

Ingredients:

- 1 can tomatoes
- 1 can tomatoes with green chilies
- ⅛ teaspoon black pepper
- ½ cup water
- ½ teaspoon cumin
- ¼ teaspoon salt
- ¾ pound ground beef
- ¼ teaspoon oregano
- ½ teaspoon chili powder
- 2 tablespoons olive oil
- 1 clove garlic
- ¾ cup uncooked white rice

- ½ medium onion

Method:

1. In a large frying pan, brown the ground beef, stirring constantly.
2. Drain the water and set it aside.
3. On moderate flame, drizzle vegetable oil into the pan.
4. Sauté onions for three minutes, or until soft.
5. Mix in the garlic and grain until the rice is finely browned.
6. Combine the ground beef, oregano, chili powder, smoked paprika, salt, black pepper, and tomatoes in a large mixing bowl.
7. Get the water to a boil.
8. Reduce to medium heat, cover, and cook for 20 minutes, or till all liquid has been absorbed.

5.9 Mediterranean Baked Tapas

Cooking Time: 15 minutes

Serving Size: 4

Ingredients:

- 3 tablespoon olive oil
- 110g sundried tomatoes
- 8 cloves garlic
- 110g chorizo sausages

Method:

1. Set the oven to 150 degrees Celsius.

2. Heat a whole clove, chorizo treats, and quasi tomato in a tiny cast-iron skillet with just a little canola oil for 2-three minutes on the hot plate.

3. Place the whole combination in the oven and continue to cook for 10-12 minutes.

4. Turn off the heat and set aside to cool moderately before brushing with the residual oil and serve with toasted bread.

5.10 Chorizo and Potato Tapas

Cooking Time: 40 minutes

Serving Size: 6

Ingredients:

- 1kg new potatoes
- 250g small cooking chorizo
- Pinch smoked paprika
- 400g can tomato
- 1 tablespoon olive oil
- 1 red chili
- Pinch cayenne pepper
- 2 garlic cloves
- 1 onion

Method:

1. In a bowl, heat a little more oil and cook the onions, garlic, and chili till the onion loosens, then mix in the smoked paprika and parmesan.

2. Bring the tomatoes to a low boil, then reduce to low heat. Season to taste and blend with a stand mixer.
3. In the meantime, steam the potato for ten minutes when slowly cooking the chorizo and releasing some of its oil in a deep fryer.
4. Remove any excess red oil and replace it with 1 tablespoon olive oil.
5. Fry all together, including the potatoes. Pour into a mixing dish.

Chapter 6: Classic Spanish Dishes

6.1 Mediterranean Skillet Chicken with Bulgur Paella, Carrots

Cooking Time: 50 minutes

Serving Size: 4

Ingredients:

Lemon Yogurt Sauce

- Pinch of cayenne pepper
- Kosher salt
- Zest and juice of 1 lemon
- 2 tablespoons curly parsley
- 1½ cups plain yogurt

For the Chicken

- ½ cup golden raisins
- ½ cup curly parsley sprigs
- 2 cups safflower oil
- ½ cup whole blanched almonds
- 6 chicken thighs
- 2 bay leaves
- 1½ cups basmati rice
- 4 whole cloves
- 2 cinnamon sticks
- 3 cups chicken stock
- 5 cardamom pods

- 6 chicken drumsticks
- 2 tablespoons tomato paste
- 3 strips orange zest
- Kosher salt and pepper
- ½ teaspoon turmeric
- 2 tomatoes
- 2 tablespoons olive oil
- 1 teaspoon cumin
- 1 teaspoon coriander
- 1 large onion
- 2 teaspoons fresh ginger
- ½ cup grated carrot
- 3 cloves garlic

Method:

1. Combine yogurt, lime juice and zest, tarragon, and smoked paprika in a medium mixing cup.
2. Put aside after seasoning with salt.
3. Preheat the oven to 375 degrees Fahrenheit.
4. Season the chicken with salt and pepper before serving.
5. Reduce the heat to medium-low and add the spices.
6. Place them skin-side up golden brown chicken in the boiling liquid and bake for 25 minutes.
7. Take the rice to a boil in a saucepan with the stored liquid ingredients over moderate flame.

8. Stir in the rice, cover, and cook on low heat until the rice is tender about 20 minutes.

6.2 One Pan Spanish Chicken and Rice Recipe with Chorizo

Cooking Time: 1 hour

Serving Size: 5

Ingredients:

For Chicken

- 3 tablespoon tomato paste
- 3 cups chicken broth
- 2 garlic cloves
- 1 large ripe tomato
- 1 ½ cup rice
- 1 large green bell pepper
- 1 medium red onion
- 4 chicken thighs
- Olive oil
- 6 oz. bulk chorizo sausage
- 4 chicken drumsticks

For Spice Rub

- 1 teaspoon black pepper
- ½ teaspoon cayenne pepper
- 1 teaspoon garlic powder
- 1 teaspoon salt
- 1 tablespoon smoked paprika

Method:
1. Soak the grain in water for a few minutes.
2. Position the rice in a bowl after thoroughly rinsing it.
3. Combine the ingredients, salt, and peppers in a small cup.
4. Dress the chicken with salt and pepper.
5. Brown both sides of the chicken.
6. Cautiously put the chicken in the pot and cook both sides thoroughly.
7. Transfer the chorizo to the same plate.
8. Combine the green beans, onions, and garlic in a large mixing bowl.
9. Cook for five minutes over a moderate flame, stirring frequently.
10. Combine the sliced tomatoes, tomato sauce, and chicken stock in a large mixing bowl.
11. Return the browned poultry to the bowl. Cook for 20 to 30 minutes at 350°F.
12. Cook the rice in the same pot as the chicken.
13. Allow the chicken and rice to rest in the pan for a few minutes.

6.3 Spanish Mixed Green Salad

Cooking Time: 10 minutes

Serving Size: 4

Ingredients:

- ½ Spanish onion
- 10 -12 green olives
- 2 cups Boston lettuce
- 2 tomatoes
- 1 cup baby spinach
- 2 cups romaine lettuce

Dressing

- 3 tablespoons olive oil
- Sea salt and black pepper
- 1 tablespoon lemon juice

Method:

1. Combine all of the dressing components in a mixing bowl and whisk until thoroughly combined.
2. Toss with salad well before eating.

6.4 Saucy Spanish Chicken with Green Olives

Cooking Time: 150 minutes

Serving Size: 8

Ingredients:

- ¼ cup sherry
- 1 tablespoon cornstarch
- 2 teaspoon dried thyme
- 1 teaspoon cumin and paprika
- 8 chicken drumsticks
- 1 small red onion
- 2 large garlic cloves
- 1 cup green olives
- 389ml can tomato sauce

Method:

1. Remove the skin from the chicken and remove any excess fat.
2. Pour the sauce in. Quantify out the artichokes, then cut them up and throw them in.
3. Combine the onion, ginger, thyme, smoked paprika, and tarragon in a mixing bowl.
4. Place the chicken in the paste to coat it, then turn it bone-side out. Push your way into the liquid.
5. Cook for six hours on medium or 2½ to 3 hours on average, or until chicken reaches 165°F.
6. Combine cornstarch and a few tablespoons of water in a mixing bowl and whisk until smooth.

7. Stir frequently in the sauce until it thickens, around five minutes. Serve chicken over rice.

6.5 Pisto

Cooking Time: 1 hour 20 minutes

Serving Size: 8

Ingredients:
- 1 teaspoon honey
- 2 medium zucchini
- 1.5 cans tomatoes
- 1.5 teaspoons salt
- 1 green bell pepper
- 2 garlic cloves
- 1 large eggplant
- ½ long red chili
- 1 red bell pepper
- Good quality olive oil
- 1 large onion
- ½ teaspoon salt

Method:
1. Spray the eggplant with salts and slice it into pieces.
2. Allow for 15-20 minutes of rest time.
3. In a big, roasting pan, heat four tablespoons of canola oil over moderate flame.
4. Combine the onions, chili, and diced beans in a large mixing bowl. Cook for 12-14 minutes over moderate flame.

5. Fry for 4-5 minutes, mixing halfway through, until the eggplant is golden brown.
6. Remove the eggplant from the pan and drizzle with a little more canola oil.
7. Cook for another 4-5 minutes after adding the zucchini.
8. Ultimately, mix in the pre-fried zucchini and eggplant to the tomatoes concentrate in the pot.
9. Cover and cook for 25 minutes over a moderate flame with a seal.

6.6 Easy Seafood Paella Recipe

Cooking Time: 1 hour

Serving Size: 6

Ingredients:
- 1 lb. prawns
- ¼ cup fresh parsley
- 2 large Roma tomatoes
- 6 oz. French green beans
- 4 small lobster tails
- ½ teaspoon chili pepper flakes
- Salt
- Water
- 1 teaspoon Spanish paprika
- 1 teaspoon cayenne pepper
- 3 tablespoon olive oil
- 4 garlic cloves
- 2 large pinches of saffron

- 2 cups Spanish rice
- 1 large yellow onion

Method:
1. Take 3 cups of water to a gentle simmer in a big saucepan.
2. Tongs are used to cut the lobster tails.
3. After 2 minutes of sautéing the onions, add the garlic and cook for another 3 minutes, stirring frequently.
4. Combine the saffron, dripping water, paprika, smoked paprika, Aleppo paprika, and salt in a mixing bowl.
5. Combine the tomato slices and green beans in a mixing bowl.
6. Cook for an additional ten minutes, just until the seafood changes color.
7. Add the cooked seafood chunks last.
8. Serve with rosemary as a garnish.
9. With your favorite white wine, eat the paella sweet.

6.7 Gambas al Ajillo

Cooking Time: 20 minutes

Serving Size: 4

Ingredients:
- 2 tablespoons dry sherry
- 1 tablespoon Italian parsley
- 1 teaspoon hot smoked paprika
- ¼ cup extra-virgin olive oil

- 1 pound shrimp
- 4 cloves garlic

Method:

1. Finely cut garlic. Paprika and sea salt are used to season the shrimp. To coat, mix it.
2. In a pan, cook the garlic and oil on moderate flame.
3. Cook for about two minutes or until the garlic begins to turn translucent.
4. Increase the heat to the extreme and add the shrimp.
5. Toss and rotate the shrimp with tongs for around two minutes or until they start to curl but are still uncooked.
6. Pour the sherry in. Heat, constantly stirring, for 1 minute more, or till sauces come to boiling and shrimp is fried through.
7. Remove the pan from the heat. With a spoon, fold in the parsley.

6.8 Easy Spanish Tortilla Recipe

Cooking Time: 50 minutes

Serving Size: 4

Ingredients:

- 8 eggs, beaten
- Handful flat-leaf parsley
- 400g waxy potatoes
- 6 garlic cloves
- 4 tablespoon olive oil

- 25g butter
- 1 large white onion

To Serve

- 4 vine tomatoes
- Drizzle of olive oil
- 1 baguette

Method:

1. Preheat a large nonstick deep fryer to medium.
2. Steadily roast the onion in the butter and oil until it is tender. Slice the tomatoes in the meantime.
3. Add the potatoes to the skillet, wrap, and cook for another 15-20 minutes, occasionally mixing to ensure even cooking.
4. Add 2 garlic cloves crushed and mixed in, followed by pounded eggs.
5. Replace the lid on the pan and bake the tortilla on low heat.
6. When the tortilla is finished, move it to a plate and eat it warm or hot, with grated parmesan on top.

6.9 Easy Spanish Garlic Soup

Cooking Time: 45 minutes

Serving Size: 4

Ingredients:

- ¼ cup flat-leaf parsley
- 4 large eggs
- 1 pinch cayenne pepper

- Salt and black pepper
- 6 cups French bread
- 1 ½ teaspoon smoked paprika
- 6 cups chicken broth
- 1 tablespoon olive oil
- 6 cloves garlic
- 2 ounces ham
- ¼ cup extra virgin olive oil

Method:
1. Preheat the oven to 350 degrees Fahrenheit.
2. Place the Sourdough bread on the baking tray that has been prepared.
3. Cook until crispy in a preheated oven.
4. In a large saucepan over medium heat, warm ¼ cup canola oil.
5. Cover and stir for 1 minute, or until ham is cooked through.
6. Cook for another minute after adding 1 to 2 teaspoons of parmesan.
7. Pour the chicken broth into the bread combination and whisk in the cayenne pepper, pepper, and garlic powder.
8. Bring to the boil, then decrease to low heat and whisk in the parsley.
9. Crack each egg into a shallow saucepan or cup.
10. With a spoon, make four downturns in the bread on the edge of the stew.
11. Pour the soup into bowls and finish with an egg.

6.10 Rustic Spanish Chicken Casserole

Cooking Time: 1 hour 20 minutes
Serving Size: 6

Ingredients:
- ½ teaspoon cayenne pepper
- 1 cup basil leaves
- 1 teaspoon dried oregano
- ½ teaspoon smoked paprika
- 1 cup stuffed pimento olives
- 1 carrot, diced
- 1 red bell pepper
- 2 tablespoon tomato paste
- 1 can cannellini beans
- ½ cup chicken stock
- 1 tablespoon olive oil
- 8 chicken thigh cutlets
- 2 cans tomatoes
- 3 garlic cloves
- 1 white onion

Method:
1. Preheat the oven to 180 degrees Celsius.
2. In a huge slow cooker, heat the oil over moderate flame.
3. For a few minutes, sauté the cloves and vegetables until they are translucent.

4. Cook for a few minutes after adding the chicken thighs.
5. With the exception of the basil leaves, combine all of the remaining ingredients in a mixing bowl.
6. 5 minutes on top of the burner, heat until softly bubbling.
7. Preheat the oven to 350°F and bake for 45 minutes on average.
8. Serve with carrots or cabbage rice.

6.11 Summer Spanish Salad

Cooking Time: 10 minutes

Serving Size: 2

Ingredients:
- 3 tablespoons olive oil
- 2 tablespoon red wine vinegar
- A pinch of cumin
- ½ teaspoon salt
- 2 large tomatoes
- 1 large green pepper
- 2 cloves garlic minced
- 1 medium onion
- 1 large cucumber

Method:
1. Dip the onions in water after cutting them into small cubes.

2. Position the tomatoes, celery, and peppers in a cup and chop them up.
3. Drain the vegetables and combine them with the remaining ingredients.
4. In a separate small cup, combine the remaining olive oil, vinegar, and salt, then stir in the garlic paste.
5. Toss the salad with the dressing and toss well.
6. Cover and store in the refrigerator.

6.12 Spanish Tuna and Potato Salad Recipe

Cooking Time: 24 minutes

Serving Size: 8

Ingredients:

- 3 tablespoon white wine vinegar
- 6 oz. spring greens
- ½ teaspoon red pepper flakes
- ⅓ cup Greek olive oil
- 1 teaspoon smoked paprika
- ¾ teaspoon cumin
- 3 large garlic cloves
- Salt and pepper
- 12 oz. fingerling potatoes
- ⅓ cup pearl red onions
- 15 oz. can quality tuna
- 6 oz. small tomatoes
- 10 oz. French green beans

Method:

1. Fill a big pot halfway with water and add the fingerling vegetables.
2. Cook for ten minutes at a low temperature.
3. Fill a wide bowl halfway with ice water and place it next to the pot.
4. Add green beans to the hot water in the same frying pan.
5. Cook for about four minutes.
6. Wash the green beans and instantly placed them in the ice water bowl.
7. Green beans, peppers, tomatoes, fish, and garlic are added to the pot.
8. Add Salt, powder, parmesan, cumin, and ground red pepper to taste.
9. Toss all together gently to ensure that all of the components are properly coated.
10. Taste and change seasoning, if necessary, by adding more smoked paprika, cilantro, or smashed red pepper.

6.13 Spanish Style Albondigas

Cooking Time: 2 hours 20 minutes

Serving Size: 4

Ingredients:

- 1 can plum tomatoes
- 2 tablespoons olive oil
- 1 cup white wine
- 2 tablespoons tomato puree
- ¼ teaspoon coriander

- 2 grinds black pepper
- ⅔ pound beef
- 1 ½ teaspoons basil
- 1 ½ teaspoons oregano
- ⅓ pound pork
- 2 tablespoons celery
- 1 clove garlic
- 2 tablespoons carrot
- 3 ½ ounces pancetta
- 3 tablespoons onion
- 3 ½ ounces white bread crumbs
- 2 tablespoons olive oil
- 2 tablespoons red bell pepper
- 2 dashes Worcestershire sauce
- Salt and pepper
- 2 tablespoons green onion
- 1 tablespoon fresh parsley
- 1 clove garlic
- 2 tablespoons fresh oregano

Method:
1. In a mixing bowl, combine ground beef, pork belly, spring onions, oregano, tarragon, garlic, Balsamic vinegar, salt, and black pepper.
2. Slowly stir in the breadcrumbs until the meat mixture reaches the perfect consistency.
3. Freezer meatballs for at least 30 minutes after wrapping them in cling film.

4. In a big saucepan, steam 2 tablespoons olive oil on medium-high heat.
5. In a hot skillet, continue cooking pancetta until it is golden brown, about four minutes. Toss in the vegetables and seasoning.
6. In a wide skillet, steam two tablespoons of oil over medium heat.
7. 6 to 10 minutes, continue cooking meatballs in hot oil quantities until uniformly browned and heated through.
8. Transfer the meatballs softly into the boiling sauce and cook together until the meatballs are thoroughly cooked.

6.14 Pontevedra-Style Spanish Chicken

Cooking Time: 1 hour 25 minutes

Serving Size: 6

Ingredients:
- ¼ cup Spanish smoked paprika
- Salt and black pepper
- ½ cup butter
- 1 head roasted garlic
- 2 cups olive oil
- 1 whole chicken

Method:
1. Preheat the oven to 350 degrees Fahrenheit.
2. Position the meat pieces skin-side up in a casserole dish.
3. Over the chicken, drizzle the sour cream and icing sugar.

4. Season the bits with salt and black pepper and chopped roasted garlic, parmesan, and tarragon.
5. Roast for thirty minutes in a dry pan.
6. Fry the chicken parts skin-side up until the chicken is cooked through and the meat is crisp.
7. Offer the chicken parts with a serving sauce on the side.

6.15 Spanish Cold Tomato Soup

Cooking Time: 25 minutes

Serving Size: 4

Ingredients:
- 2 hardboiled eggs
- Diced serrano ham
- A splash of sherry vinegar
- A pinch of salt
- 8 medium tomatoes
- 1 cup olive oil again
- 1 clove of garlic
- 1 medium baguette

Method:
1. Carry a big pot of salted water to a boil on the burner.
2. In the base of each tomato, make a small symbol.
3. Remove the cores from the tomatoes and mix everything else.
4. Use a high-powered blender, combine all ingredients.

5. Remove the "guts" from your baguette and toss them in with the blended vegetables.
6. Mix in the drop of vinegar, pepper, and garlic until the soup has even consistency.
7. Mix in 1 hardboiled egg until completely combined.
8. Offer in big containers with toppings of diced poblano pepper and diced ham. Serve chilled.

6.16 Spicy Spanish Meatballs

Cooking Time: 35 minutes

Serving Size: 4

Ingredients:

Spanish Meatballs

- 2 ½ teaspoon smoked paprika
- ¼ cup olive oil
- 2 clove garlic
- 1 egg yolk
- 2 tablespoon milk
- 500 grams beef
- ½ cup breadcrumbs

Smoked Paprika Tomato Sauce

- ½ teaspoon smoked paprika
- 500 grams tomatoes
- 3 cloves garlic
- 1 bay leaf
- 1 onion

- 1 tablespoon olive oil

Method:

1. Soak the breadcrumbs in dairy for five minutes before pressing out any remaining water.
2. Add salt and pepper to taste.
3. Make 12 balls out of the flour mix and place them on a table to work with.
4. In a large skillet, heat the oil over medium heat.
5. Heat the meatballs for four minutes, rotating once or until golden brown.
6. Heat for about four minutes with the spray of excess oil, onions, ginger, and bay leaf.
7. Wait for another minute till the paprika is aromatic.
8. Transfer the meatballs to the bowl after stirring in the tomatoes.
9. Transfer to a serving bowl and serve right away.

6.17 Sizzling Spanish Garlic Prawns

Cooking Time: 13 minutes

Serving Size: 6

Ingredients:

- 6 garlic cloves
- 6 tablespoons dry sherry
- 1 teaspoon chili flakes
- 4 tablespoons olive oil
- 3 tablespoons parsley
- 900g raw king prawns

Method:

1. Preheat the oven to 220 degrees Celsius.
2. Cut the prawns lengthwise but not through it and cut the vein to flap the shrimp.
3. Use six small oven tray dishes or one big one to separate the shrimp, garlic, chili or pimento, brandy, and balsamic vinegar.
4. Cook for 12 to 15 minutes until it is red and piping hot, based on the pan or pots' size.
5. Serve with toasted bread and citrus wedges, garnished with parsley.

6.18 Super Tasty Spanish Roast Chicken

Cooking Time: 1 hour 40 minutes

Serving Size: 8

Ingredients:
- Olive oil
- 2 cloves garlic
- Freshly ground black pepper
- 300g Iberico chorizo sausage
- 2kg chicken
- Sea salt
- 1.6kg potatoes
- 1 handful parsley
- 4 lemons

Method:
1. Heat your oven to 220°C, and put your vegetables in a large pan of boiling water containing two lemons and simmer for five minutes.

2. Take the leaves from the tarragon stalks and set them aside.
3. Fill the meat with the tarragon stalks and warm lemons.
4. Position the potato in the center of the baking parchment, then the poultry on top and the pancetta on top of that.
5. Whereas the chicken and vegetables are frying, make the gremolata, as the Italians name it.
6. Chop the poultry and serve with the potatoes on eight plates.

6.19 Spanish-Inspired Tomato Salad

Cooking Time: 40 minutes

Serving Size: 8

Ingredients:

- 16 caper berries
- 6 anchovy fillets
- 3 pounds tomatoes
- 1 cup parsley
- ½ teaspoon sugar
- ¼ teaspoon salt
- 1/3 cup olive oil
- 3 tablespoons sherry vinegar
- 1 teaspoon pepper
- 1 teaspoon paprika
- 1 cup fresh breadcrumbs
- 5 cloves garlic

Method:
1. In a large saucepan, warm 1/3 cup oil over moderate flame.
2. Cook, occasionally stirring, for about 20 seconds, just until the citrus is spicy and piping hot but not crispy.
3. In the same pan, heat and cook two tablespoons of oil over moderate flame.
4. Cook, constantly stirring, until the breadcrumbs are crisp and lightly browned, about five minutes.
5. In a mixing bowl, combine the garlic-paprika oil, mustard, spice, cinnamon, and salt.
6. Gently whisk in the onions, tarragon, caper fruit, and minced anchovies.
7. Serve the tomato salad on a large plate with the fried cornmeal on top.

6.20 Fruity Spanish Tapas

Cooking Time: 30 minutes

Serving Size: 4

Ingredients:
- 50g vegetarian manchego
- 1 tablespoon chives
- 1 tablespoon garlic oil
- 1 Pink Lady apple
- ¼ ciabatta

Method:
1. Trim the edges of the ciabatta blocks so they sit flat on a surface.
2. Heat a baking tray to a high temperature.

3. Grill the ciabatta pieces for 2-3 minutes, rotating once, until finely charred all over.
4. Remove the board from the oven and place it on top of it.
5. Heat for 2-3 minutes, rotating halfway, till the apple slices are slightly charred.
6. To combine, place two slices of fruit, a cheese slice, and a sprinkling of chives on each cube of bread.
7. Serve after securing with a toothpick.

Conclusion

Tapas can be eaten in a variety of ways. You'll probably wind up buying a lot of small dishes and exchanging them when you go out for tapas. This route, you can sample a variety of dishes at once. Tapas are small plates of meals available with small pieces of bread, and they reflect the best fresh foods from different parts of Spain in Madrid. Poblano Jamón Tapas are distinctive to each country. Queso manchego (a spreadable cheese in Spain's La Mancha area) is common in the southern coast center, while tapas with la morcilla (sausage) is popular in the north. Tapas can typically cost from 50 cents to four euros, based on the tapa. Even with the same tapa, prices vary based on the jamón (ham) location you request. Tapas are the nutrition purgatory; they are there to fill in the holes in your day. It does not complement or substitute for a meal, apart from an appetizer. They are sold at Tasca bars, where people indulge in these delicacies before lunch or dinner. Tapas would most probably be served in the evenings before dinners when you visit Spain. The excitement and the delicious food and drinks will hold you for more. So give these tapas ideas a try, and you'll fall in love with the flavor of these delectable tapas.

TAPAS
COOKBOOK

70 Easy Recipes for Preparing Traditional Food from Spain

Maki Blanc

© **Copyright 2021 by Maki Blanc - All rights reserved.**

This document is geared towards providing exact and reliable information in regards to the topic and issue covered. The publication is sold with the idea that the publisher is not required to render accounting, officially permitted, or otherwise, qualified services. If advice is necessary, legal or professional, a practiced individual in the profession should be ordered.

- From a Declaration of Principles which was accepted and approved equally by a Committee of the American Bar Association and a Committee of Publishers and Associations.

It is not legal in any way to reproduce, duplicate, or transmit any part of this document in either electronic means or in printed format. Recording of this publication is strictly prohibited and any storage of this document is not allowed unless with written permission from the publisher. All rights reserved.

The information provided herein is stated to be truthful and consistent, in that any liability, in terms of inattention or otherwise, by any usage or abuse of any policies, processes, or directions contained within is the solitary and utter responsibility of the recipient reader. Under no circumstances will any legal responsibility or blame be held against the publisher for any reparation, damages, or monetary loss due to the information herein, either directly or indirectly.

Respective authors own all copyrights not held by the publisher.

The information herein is offered for informational purposes solely, and is universal as so. The presentation of the information is without contract or any type of guarantee assurance.

The trademarks that are used are without any consent, and the publication of the trademark is without permission or backing by the trademark owner. All trademarks and brands within this book are for clarifying purposes only and are the owned by the owners themselves, not affiliated with this document.

Introduction

Tapas describes the way food is served rather than individual dishes. This is not to say that there are not popular tapas dishes to be found in any respectable tapas bar. To begin with, a "tapa" is merely a small serving of food. Tapas can be eaten in a variety of ways. You'll probably wind up buying a lot of small dishes and exchanging them when you go out for tapas. This route, you can sample a variety of dishes at once. The most popular origin story for tapas is that they began as tiny slices of meats or toast served in cafes as a way for drinkers to keep flies away from their beverages. The Spanish word tapas means "to cover." Gradually, the tiny bar snack became just as important as the beverages. They began to become more elaborate as well.

There are a few other hypotheses on how the title came to be, but no one knows for sure. Tapas are believed to have originated in the provinces of Andalusia in southern Spain, and the practice is centuries old. Tapas have spread across Spain and have become an important part of their culture, as tapas have developed alongside Spanish food culture. Tapas are divided into three categories: pinchos, cosas de picar, and cazuelas. Tiny foods such as artichokes and Jamon are known as Cosas de picar. Pinchos are tapas that come with a chopstick, such as a slice of Spain flatbread fixed to a loaf of toast with a toothpick. Cazuelas are specialty pizzas of food with salsa and a bit more material, such as grilled shrimp, sausages, or even a whole Spanish flatbread.

Tapas are small plates of meals available with small pieces of bread, and they reflect the best fresh foods from different parts of Spain in Madrid. Poblano Jamón Tapas are distinctive to each country.

Queso manchego (a spreadable cheese in Spain's La Mancha area) is common in the southern coast center, while tapas with la morcilla (sausage) is popular in the north. Tapas can typically cost from 50 cents to four euros, based on the tapa. Even with the same tapa, prices vary based on the jamón (ham) location you request.

Tapas are the nutrition purgatory; they are there to fill in the holes in your day. It does not complement or substitute for a meal, apart from an appetizer. They are sold at Tasca bars, where people indulge in these delicacies before lunch or dinner. Tapas would most probably be served in the evenings before dinners when you visit Spain. "Tapas Cookbook" has a wide range of Tapas and Spanish recipes with different ingredients and methods. It has six chapters based on Breakfast, snack, lunch, dinner, salad, soups, and side's recipes. The fifth chapter is about classic Spanish recipes, and six chapters are dedicated to vegetarian recipes. All recipes with lots of health benefits are here. Try these recipes and make your meal more delightful and flavorful.

Chapter 1: Getting Started with Spanish Food

Traditional Spanish food is simple, unpretentious food made with locally sourced ingredients or staple crops in the area. Mountains pass through Spain in many ways, creating natural access barriers and rendering transportation impossible until the second half of the twentieth century. This is only one of the factors why cooking varies so much from place to place. The other is that Spain was formed by the union of several independent kingdoms with its customs.

Most dishes are now cooked using the same techniques and products as they had been two or three centuries ago. The Arabs who invaded and lived in Spain for over eight hundred years, like the Romans, made significant contributions to Traditional dishes, as seen in many dishes. Other dishes arose as a result of American and European factors and were then adjusted to Spanish preferences. A few things have not changed: The food in Spain is clean, plentiful, and flavorful, and the Spaniards adore it.

1.1 History of Spanish Food

Spaniards, such as the Germans and the French, are adamant that their cuisine is the finest in the world. Despite the heated debate, many foreign foodies and critics succeed. Spain is known around the world for its wine, artichokes, olives, Iberico Jamun, pickled veggies, as well as, of course, tapas.

Spain's place, especially in the Atlantic Ocean and the Mediterranean Sea, has influenced its cuisine. In traditional Spanish recipes, salmon is abundant and common.

The several foreign locations that Spain once invaded have also had a strong influence on Traditional dishes. For example, Arabic crops such as grain, cocoa beans, auberge, peanuts, and lemon are frequently used in Spanish cuisine.

Spain ruled several parts of South America during the arrival of the new era. They finally brought a range of foods from South America, including onions, tomatoes, peas, and cocoa. At the period, Spanish cuisine was still evolving, incorporating products from all over the world. The Spanish, surprisingly, were using tomatoes in their cuisine. Since tomatoes are similar to the coffee plant, Europeans originally thought they were poisonous. Spaniards started to integrate the then-unfamiliar "plant" into their food cultures after discovering that tomatoes are not toxic and were, in reality, tasty and healthy.

1.2 History of Traditional Dishes from Spain

The Romans donated olive oil and liquor, the Arabs donated various gazpachos, water systems, nuts, and a variety of other famous and now traditional products, the ollas we currently know would not have been feasible without their Prayer celebration and unique process conditions, and one of Spain's main competitors, ham, will not be amongst these best in the world if it weren't for Christians. Cocoas, in general, are one of those products that have influenced global eating habits. Where would we be if it weren't for cocoa? This snack became so famous around the world due to Spain's healthy appetite. Plus, they mixed it with other flavors such delicacies as caramel con churros and Atletico favorite.

Spain has a long agricultural history that includes a diverse variety of nutrients. It is one of the world's leading suppliers of grape and artichokes, in general.

Both of these ingredients are used in the production of two of Spain's most popular products: liquor and olives. Various Classifications of Source now cover both of these items. Spanish cuisine is still developing today, and it is one of the pioneers in developing a healthy balanced diet.

1.3 Health Benefits of Spanish Food

Food material from the area's rugged terrain is emphasized in Spanish cuisine. Small plates of high-quality products, as well as salmon and veggies, are popular. While rich foods like Iberico ham and serrano ham are available, Spain also offers various lighter and healthy options. There is no such thing as a calorie-restricted plan in Spain. Its world-famous Mediterranean diet emphasizes a high intake of vegetables, berries, peanuts, grains, and fish, as well as plenty of olive oil, reasonable dairy intake, and a low intake of red meat. At meals, it is often common to drink that little wine professionally.

The Spanish place a premium on spending time with family and friends while still staying physically involved. It's an integral part of their everyday routine and a tradition as significant as football. Since food is considered sacred and intended to be appreciated, the Spanish do not limit themselves to calorie counting, fatty grams, or fructose intake to determine moderation.

The Spanish food is heart-healthy, which may clarify why Spain has one of the lower heart disease rates. The diet can help with weight loss comfortably due to its emphasis on the whole, healthy produce. It's not for a quick fix, but it's a good eating habit to develop long-term results. The Spanish eating healthy style helps avoid gestational diabetes and is an ideal way to manage and regulate blood sugar levels. Certain aspects of the diet, such as its high anti-inflammatory omega-3 fats, seem to help alleviate RA symptoms.

The modest olive occupies a central position in Spanish cuisine. You're doing your body a favor by consuming raw olives or raining extra virgin olive oil across toasted bread and vegetables. Olives are high in monounsaturated fats, which lower cardiovascular disease risk and increase HDL cholesterol levels. Olives do have anti-inflammatory and antioxidant activities, which means they can help prevent diseases and cancers.

Spain is a nation with a long and diverse coastline. It is the ruler of a Mediterranean Ocean and North Atlantic territory. As a result, a ton of fish appears on Spanish lists. The anchovy, a sweetness full of Omega-3 fats, Vitamin b, magnesium, and phosphorus, is most common. Many anchovies are wrapped in salt, which can be washed away with water.

This small legume is dense, high in fiber, and has a spicy flavor. They're also very cheap, that's why they're used in so many rural recipes in Spain. Lentils provide 63 percent of your daily soluble fiber needs in just one cup. This aids in the regulation of blood sugar, metabolism, and losing weight. Lentils often include phosphorus and magnesium, all of which are beneficial to cardiovascular health.

Almonds are a heart-healthy treat that can be used in a variety of Spanish sweets and recipes. They're high in manganese, folic acid, and copper, all of which your body requires to turn energy from food. They also have a low glycemic index, making them a good way to keep blood sugar levels stable. The fact that they are rich in saturated fats is their best feature. If you really need to lower your blood sugar levels, this means they are indeed a heart-healthy option to processed meats.

1.4 Preparing Ingredients for Spanish Dishes

Olive oil and cloves are the two most basic materials in Spanish cuisine; in reality, cloves and olive oil are frequently the only products used in the region. However, since Spain is made up of various geographical areas inhabited by various ethnic and religious backgrounds, and because the climate differs from region to region, dominant cultures are diverse.

The following is a list of popular components and foods:

Olive oil: Spain is a major producer of olive oil, and olive trees can be found in the Andalusia area in the southern part of the country. Olive oil is used for frying a lot of traditional Spanish dishes.

Seafood and salmon: Since Spain is situated on the Iberian Peninsula, local fish is often available in markets and cafes.

Poultry is a very common dish. It can be prepared in a variety of ways, but the most popular are frying or simmered, while roasted chicken can be purchased "to go" in many smaller shops.

Cheeses: Spain has a wide variety of delicious cheeses made from cow, goat, dairy, and blended milk.

Beef, pork, and lamb are all traditional cuts of meat that can be roasted, fried over charcoal, or sautéed in a sauce.

Sausages: The Spanish adore sausage, particularly chorizo, a paprika-infused pork sausage. Chorizo comes in a variety of flavors, from clean and fluffy to charred and aged.

Cloves, tomatoes, and herbs like thyme, cardamom, and rosemary are all used, but garlic is used more than others.

Ham, or jamón in Spanish, is a valued delicacy. Spaniards are passionate about their ham and would pay a premium for the best.

Eggs: Eggs are consumed on a regular basis, whether fried, mashed potatoes, or in a Spanish omelet known as a tortilla Espaola.

Nuts: Almonds, walnuts, and hazelnuts are among Spain's main exports. Desserts made with almonds and milk are very popular.

In view of food, Spain is still one of the most popular nations in the world. Spain has evolved into one of the world's first and most influential "fusion" delicacies.

Chapter 2: Tapas Breakfast, Snacks, and Appetizers

2.1 Fried Chorizo with Chick Peas and Tomatoes

Cooking Time: 20 minutes

Serving Size: 4

Ingredients:

- Salt and pepper
- 3 tablespoons parsley
- 2 pints cherry tomatoes
- 1 teaspoon smoked paprika
- 9 ounces chorizo
- 2 15-oz. cans chickpeas
- 1 onion
- 1 tablespoon olive oil

Method:

8. In a saucepan over medium heat, steam the oil.
9. Sauté onion for three minutes, or until soft.
10. Toss in the chorizo.
11. Sauté for 30 seconds to 1 minute, or until thoroughly hot.
12. Combine chickpeas, grape tomatoes, and paprika in a mixing bowl.
13. Cook for 8 minutes, or until tomatoes are softened, and liquids are boiling.

14. Salt and pepper to taste. Serve with a tarragon garnish.

2.2 Boquerones Al Limon

Cooking Time: 30 minutes

Serving Size: 2

Ingredients:

- Chickpea flour
- Salt
- 1 clove of garlic
- 1 bunch of parsley
- 1 lemon
- 350 grams anchovies

Method:

11. The anchovies should be cleaned and dried.
12. Place the garlic, tarragon, and pepper in a mortar and use the pestle to grind them into a powder.
13. Combine the paste with the extract of one lemon.
14. Place the fillets in a crystal tray and spill the marinade over them.
15. Cover the plate with plastic wrap and refrigerate for up to two hours to soak.
16. Take off the extra chickpea flour after passing them through.
17. In a large pan, heat some butter over medium heat.
18. Fry 4-5 at the moment for 1 minute, or till they transform a lovely golden color.

19. To absorb excess oil, place the fried fish on a plate lined with towels.

20. Serve with lime wedges and aioli sauce.

2.3 Spanish Churros and Chocolate

Cooking Time: 45 minutes

Serving Size: 14

Ingredients:

For the Cinnamon Sugar
- 2 tablespoons granulated sugar
- 1 teaspoon cinnamon

For the Chocolate Sauce
- 1 cup semisweet chocolate
- 1 ¼ cups heavy cream

For the Churros Dough
- 1 cup all-purpose flour
- Vegetable oil
- ½ teaspoon kosher salt
- 2 tablespoons vegetable oil
- 2½ tablespoons sugar
- 1 cup water

Method:

11. Mix the sugars and spices in a small bowl and stir to blend.

12. Add the cream to a pot over medium heat. Get it to a low simmer.

13. Put the cocoa in a heatproof cup, add the hot butter over it, and cover the bucket in cling film.
14. Combine the sugar, salt, and soybean oil in a mixing bowl.
15. Get the water to a boil, then turn off the steam.
16. Mix in the flour until it creates a creamy sauce.
17. In a skillet, add the oil to 375°F over moderate flame.
18. Deep-fry for four minutes, or until golden, nicely browned.
19. Toss with the cinnamon and sugar right away.
20. With the white chocolate, serve hot or at ambient temperature.

2.4 Basque Breakfast Sandwich

Cooking Time: 20 minutes

Serving Size: 8

Ingredients:
- 8 eggs
- ¼ cup fresh parsley
- ¼ cup (60 ml) beer
- 8 thick slices of baguette
- 1 large white onion
- 2 large chorizo sausages
- ¼ cup (60 ml) olive oil

Method:

10. Heat 1½ tablespoons vegetable oil in a frying pan over medium heat.
11. Heat, frequently stirring, for 2-three minutes, or till onions begin to soften.
12. Mix in the chorizo and bake for another 4-five minutes.
13. Bake the sliced baguette in the oven for 1-2 minutes on each side until it's lightly browned.
14. Heat and cook canola oil in the same bowl.
15. Working in batches of 2 to 4, smash eggs into the skillet and stir for approximately 3 minutes, or until target doneness is reached.
16. Toasted baguette slices should be topped with the onion-chorizo mixture.
17. Season the eggs with salt and pepper before placing one cooked egg on each piece of toast.
18. Continue with the left eggs. Serve the toasts with chopped parsley on top.

2.5 Spicy Crab Salad Tapas

Cooking Time: 35 minutes

Serving Size: 10

Ingredients:
- 1 large egg
- 1 tablespoon water
- ¼ teaspoon pepper
- 1 package pastry
- 1 can lump crabmeat
- ½ cup mayonnaise

- ½ teaspoon salt
- ¼ cup sweet red pepper
- 2 garlic cloves
- 1 teaspoon mustard
- ¼ cup sweet yellow pepper
- 1 tablespoon cilantro
- 1 tablespoon lemon juice
- 1 jalapeno pepper
- ¼ cup green onions

Method:

11. Preheat the oven to 375 degrees Fahrenheit.
12. Mix the first twelve ingredients in a mixing bowl.
13. Refrigerate for at least 1 hour, sealed.
14. In the meantime, roll out puff pastry on a lightly floured.
15. Every pastry should be rolled into a 10-inch square and cut into twenty-five 2-inch squares.
16. Brush pastry with a mixture of egg and water.
17. Position cutout pieces on top of strong squares and move to bake sheets lined with parchment paper.
18. Bake for eighteen minutes, or until lightly browned.
19. Bring to room temperature before serving.
20. Place 1 heaping tablespoon of smoked salmon in the center of each cooked pastry once it has cooled.

2.6 Mini Spanish Omelets

Cooking Time: 35 minutes

Serving Size: 12

> **Ingredients:**
> - 75g chorizo sausage
> - 6 large eggs
> - 300g new potatoes
> - 1 small red onion
> - 2 tablespoon olive oil

Method:

11. Heat the oven to 180 degrees Celsius.
12. To remove stains, clean the potatoes thoroughly under water flow.
13. Cook whole potato for ten minutes, or until almost over.
14. In the meantime, finely cut the chorizo sausage and slice and thinly cut the spring onions.
15. In a large skillet, heat the remaining oil and cook the onions and chorizo for a few moments, just until the onion is tender.
16. Cook for another two minutes after adding the potato.
17. Split the potato mixture evenly among the muffin tins in twelve holes.
18. Break the whites into a jug or a cup and whisk them together.
19. Preheat the oven to 350°F and bake for twenty minutes, or until crispy and puffy.

20. Allow cooling for several minutes in the tin until serving hot with a greenery salad.

2.7 Zucchini Tapas Omelet

Cooking Time: 50 minutes

Serving Size: 4

Ingredients:

- 1 cebolla
- Oil and salt
- 3 potatoes
- 2 zucchini
- 6 eggs

Method:

6. Peel and rinse the potato and zucchini thoroughly before slicing them thinly.
7. In a mixing bowl, combine all of the ingredients, sprinkle with salt, and thoroughly combine.
8. While the pan is heating up, beat the eggs with a pinch of salt in a separate cup. When the oven is ready, add eggs.
9. Cook once the outside is crispy, but the inside is moist.
10. You may leave it curdled or less curdled, depending on your preference.

2.8 Roasted Vegetable Tapas

Cooking Time: 35 minutes

Serving Size: 8

Ingredients:
- Small handful parsley
- ½ teaspoon paprika
- Zest 0.5 lemon
- 8 basil leaves
- 1 large aubergine
- 25g parmesan
- 3 sundried tomatoes
- 1 large courgette
- 3 tablespoon olive oil
- 250g tub ricotta
- 1 garlic clove
- 2 flame-roasted peppers

Method:

8. Slice the aubergine and courgette onto small, 2-3mm-thick slices. The peppers should be drained and rinsed.
9. Preheat a griddle pan to medium-high heat.
10. Pour the garlic oil on the vegetable strips and roast for 2-3 minutes on each side until it's soft and finely charred.
11. Combine the cheeses, sundried tomato, lime juice, and spice in a mixing bowl.
12. Arrange the aubergine strips on a big cutting board.

13.   A strip of courgette, a slice of spice, and basil leaves go on top of each.
14.   Organize on a plate and top with parsley leaf and paprika when ready to eat.

2.9 Pan con Tomate

Cooking Time: 7 minutes

Serving Size: 8

Ingredients:
- 2 medium cloves garlic
- Flaky sea salt
- 1 loaf ciabatta
- Extra-virgin olive oil
- Kosher salt
- 2 large tomatoes

Method:

9. Tomatoes should be cut in half vertically. In a big mixing bowl, grate a box grinder.
10. Preheat the broiler to high and position the rack four inches below it.
11. Spoonful olive oil over the cut side of the bread on a work surface.
12. Use kosher salt, season to taste.
13. Position the bread cutting side up on a rack set in a pan or immediately on the griddle rack and broil for two or three minutes, or until crispy and beginning to char form around edge.
14. Take the bread from the microwave and scrub it with the garlic cloves that have been cut.
15. Spread the tomato mixture on top of the pizza.
16. Dress with flaky sesame oil and rain of extra-virgin canola oil.

2.10 Cucumber Tapas

Cooking Time: 30 minutes

Serving Size: 4

Ingredients:
- Pinch of black pepper
- 1 tablespoon oregano
- 2 ounces feta cheese
- ¼ teaspoon salt
- 2 tablespoons olive oil
- 1 teaspoon sherry vinegar
- 2 cucumbers

Method:
7. Remove the seeds from cucumbers by slicing them lengthwise.
8. 1 cucumber half should be diced into ¼-inch pieces and placed in a small cup.
9. Toss in the canola oil, mustard, feta cheese, pepper, and spice to mix. Toss in the oregano and toss once more.
10. Remove 1 or 2 thin pieces of peel from underneath each cucumber half with a potato peeler so they don't tip over.
11. Distribute the cucumber-and-feta combination between them.
12. Cut cucumbers into 1 ½-inch piece on a slight triangular and serve right away.

2.11 Spanish Tapas Platter

Cooking Time: 1 hour 15 minutes

Serving Size: 8

Ingredients:
- 2 cups green grapes
- 1 crusty loaf of bread
- 1 cup redskin Spanish peanuts
- 8 ounces fig spread
- 3.75 ounce can of sardines
- 4 ounces cheddar
- 1 cup Spanish olives pitted
- 3 ounces salami
- 4 ounces manchego
- 4 ounces prosciutto
- 4 ounces tavern ham
- 3 ounces sausage
- 3 ounces serrano ham

Method:

8. In separate bowls, position the olives, almonds, and fig scatter.
9. In a serving dish or shallow cup, position the sardines.
10. Organize the sardines on the large plate, along with the bowls of artichokes, nuts, and figs. Allow plenty of space between them.
11. After this, on the large plate, organize the meat and the Iberico cheese to fill the majority of the large area.
12. Grape bunches, cheese crackers, and sandwich slices may be used to fill up the gaps.

13. To make it easier to reach the objects, keep them close but not too near together.

14. Place the leftover bread in a bucket near the stove.

2.12 Magdalenas: Spanish Lemon Cupcakes

Cooking Time: 1 hour

Serving Size: 10

Ingredients:
- 1 tablespoon baking powder
- Pinch salt
- 1 teaspoon vanilla extract
- 1 1/3 cups pastry flour
- 3 large eggs
- ¼ cup milk
- Zest from 1 lemon
- ½ cup extra virgin olive oil
- ½ cup granulated sugar

Method:

11. Add the eggs to a big mixing bowl until bright and powdery.

12. Slowly incorporate the sugar, then the olive oil and milk.

13. Combine the lemon zest and vanilla essence in a mixing bowl.

14. Mix in the flour, icing sugar, and salt until there are no chunks.

15. Put it in the fridge for thirty minutes after covering the dish.

16. Preheat the oven to 425 degrees Fahrenheit.
17. Two-thirds of the batter should be used in each muffin container, and sugar can be sprinkled on top if needed.
18. Decrease the heat to 400 degrees Fahrenheit and position it in the oven.
19. Cook the Magdalenas for 13-fifteen minutes, or until raised and translucent from around edges.
20. Warm or at ambient temperature is perfect.

2.13 Pulpo Gallego: A Galician-Style Octopus Tapas

Cooking Time: 40 minutes

Serving Size: 4

Ingredients:

- Spanish smoked paprika
- Extra virgin olive oil
- 500g of potatoes
- Sea salt flakes
- 1 whole octopus

Method:

8. Once the water starts to boil, bring a big pot of water on the stove with a grain of salt.
9. On medium-high heat, roast your octopus for 15 to 20 minutes.
10. Ensure that the octopus remains submerged in water during the cooking process.
11. Octopus, like spaghetti, must be al dente.

12. Enable the octopus to rest throughout the liquid ingredients for a few minutes after it has finished cooking.

13. Break the octopus tentacles and vegetables into ½ inch thick slices to eat.

14. Table salt, cayenne pepper, and a healthy drizzle of olive oil complete the dish.

2.14 Spanish Tapas Toast with Escalivada

Cooking Time: 15 minutes

Serving Size: 4

Ingredients:

- Flat-leaf parsley
- Sea salt
- 80g soft goat's cheese
- 1 slice Serrano ham
- ½ jar of Escalivada
- Green olives
- Extra virgin olive oil
- 1 large bruschetta bread

Method:

7. After toasting one side of the bruschetta crust, sprinkle the uncooked side with olive oil.
8. Drain the escalivada with a fork.
9. Place the whole or doubled olives on top, then sprinkle the goat's cheese on top.
10. Put the toast back under the flame.
11. Blow the Spicy salami into small pieces and sprinkle them on top.
12. Cut into chunks or half and serve hot with a side dish of finely chopped flat-leaf parsley and sea salt pinch.

Chapter 3: Tapas Lunch, Soups and Salad

3.1 Easy Spanish Garlic Soup

Cooking Time: 45 minutes

Serving Size: 4

Ingredients:

- ¼ cup flat-leaf parsley
- 4 large eggs
- 1 pinch cayenne pepper
- Salt and black pepper
- 6 cups French bread
- 1 ½ teaspoon smoked paprika
- 6 cups chicken broth
- 1 tablespoon olive oil
- 6 cloves garlic
- 2 ounces ham
- ¼ cup extra virgin olive oil

Method:

12. Preheat the oven to 350 degrees Fahrenheit.
13. Place the Sourdough bread on the baking tray that has been prepared.
14. Cook until crispy in a preheated oven.
15. In a large saucepan over medium heat, warm ¼ cup canola oil.

16. Cover and stir for 1 minute, or until ham is cooked through.
17. Cook for another minute after adding 1 to 2 teaspoons of parmesan.
18. Pour the chicken broth into the bread combination and whisk in the cayenne pepper, pepper, and garlic powder.
19. Bring to the boil, then decrease to low heat and whisk in the parsley.
20. Each egg should be cracked into a shallow saucepan or cup.
21. With a spoon, make four downturns in the bread on the edge of the stew.
22. Pour the soup into bowls and finish with an egg.

3.2 Garlic Soup with Egg and Croutons

Cooking Time: 35 minutes

Serving Size: 2

Ingredients:

- ¼ cup extra virgin olive oil
- Salt and pepper
- 1 teaspoon sweet paprika
- 1-liter chicken broth
- 2 eggs
- 6 garlic cloves

- 2 slices of stale bread

Method:

10. Garlic should be peeled and cut into strips.
11. Heat the olive oil in a saucepan over medium heat.
12. Add garlic and cook for 2-3 minutes, or until it starts to brown.
13. Add the loaf to the pan and fry it with the garlic, allowing it to soak up the oil.
14. Reduce to low heat and stir in the parmesan.
15. Put in the liquid and give it a good swirl.
16. Take the soup to a rolling simmer, reduce to low heat, and continue cooking for about thirty minutes.
17. To taste, season with salt and pepper, using at least ½ teaspoon pepper.
18. In a large mixing bowl, whisk together the eggs and add them to the soup.

3.3 Salmorejo (Spanish Cold Tomato Soup)

Cooking Time: 25 minutes

Serving Size: 4

Ingredients:
- 2 hardboiled eggs
- Diced serrano ham
- A splash of sherry vinegar
- A pinch of salt
- 8 medium tomatoes

- 1 cup olive oil again
- 1 clove of garlic
- 1 medium baguette

Method:

9. Carry a big pot of salted water to a boil on the burner.
10. In the base of each tomato, make a small symbol.
11. Remove the cores from the tomatoes and mix everything else.
12. Use a high-powered blender, combine all ingredients.
13. Remove the "guts" from your baguette and toss them in with the blended vegetables.
14. Mix in the drop of vinegar, pepper, and garlic until the soup has even consistency.
15. Mix in 1 hardboiled egg until completely combined.
16. Offer in big containers with toppings of diced poblano pepper and diced ham. Serve chilled.

3.4 Chorizo and Potato Tapas

Cooking Time: 40 minutes

Serving Size: 6

Ingredients:

- 1kg new potatoes
- 250g small cooking chorizo
- Pinch smoked paprika
- 400g can tomato
- 1 tablespoon olive oil
- 1 red chili
- Pinch cayenne pepper
- 2 garlic cloves
- 1 onion

Method:

6. In a bowl, heat a little more oil and cook the onions, garlic, and chili till the onion loosens, then mix in the smoked paprika and parmesan.
7. Bring the tomatoes to a low boil, then reduce to low heat. Season to taste and blend with a stand mixer.
8. In the meantime, steam the potato for ten minutes when slowly cooking the chorizo and releasing some of its oil in a deep fryer.
9. Remove any excess red oil and replace it with 1 tablespoon olive oil.
10. Fry all together, including the potatoes. Pour into a mixing dish.

3.5 Spanish Tapas-Style Green Pepper

Cooking Time: 5 minutes
Serving Size: 2

Ingredients:

- 2 tablespoon olive oil
- Pinch of sea salt flakes
- 250g green peppers

Method:
6. Wipe down the peppers in ice water.
7. In a big nonstick roasting tray, heat the oil.
8. Cook the peppers for 4-5 minutes, or till their surfaces peel and become brown.
9. To drain, place them on some paper towels.
10. Serve promptly with a pinch of sea salt.

3.6 Pontevedra-Style Spanish Chicken

Cooking Time: 1 hour 25 minutes
Serving Size: 6

Ingredients:

- ¼ cup Spanish smoked paprika
- Salt and black pepper
- ½ cup butter
- 1 head roasted garlic
- 2 cups olive oil
- 1 whole chicken

Method:

8. Preheat the oven to 350 degrees Fahrenheit.
9. Position the meat pieces skin-side up in a casserole dish.
10. Over the chicken, drizzle the sour cream and icing sugar.
11. Season the bits with salt and black pepper and chopped roasted garlic, parmesan, and tarragon.
12. Roast for thirty minutes in a dry pan.
13. Fry the chicken parts skin-side up until the chicken is cooked through and the meat is crisp.
14. Offer the chicken parts with a serving sauce on the side.

3.7 Mediterranean Baked Tapas

Cooking Time: 15 minutes

Serving Size: 4

Ingredients:

- 3 tablespoon olive oil
- 110g sundried tomatoes
- 8 cloves garlic
- 110g chorizo sausages

Method:

5. Set the oven to 150 degrees Celsius.
6. Heat a whole clove, chorizo treats, and quasi tomato in a tiny cast-iron skillet with just a little canola oil for 2-three minutes on the hot plate.
7. Place the whole combination in the oven and continue to cook for 10-12 minutes.

8. Turn off the heat and set aside to cool moderately before brushing with the residual oil and serve with toasted bread.

3.8 Chicken Tapas with Romesco Sauce

Cooking Time: 50 minutes
Serving Size: 4

Ingredients:
- 2 garlic cloves
- Sea salt and pepper
- 2 tablespoon extra-virgin olive oil
- 3 sprigs of thyme
- 12 chicken thighs

For the Romesco Sauce
- ½ teaspoon of smoked paprika
- Salt and pepper to taste
- 1 tablespoon sherry vinegar
- ½ teaspoon of cumin seeds
- 2 whole red peppers
- 12 whole hazelnuts, skin off
- 6 tablespoon olive oil
- 2 ripe tomatoes
- 1 garlic clove
- 12 Marcona almonds
- 1 piece of stale bread

Method:
11. Preheat the grill on your stove.

12. Position the peppers halves on a plate, skin cut side.

13. Take the steaks from the barbecue and cover them with a kitchen towel. Peppers should be cut into large pieces.

14. To create the romesco salsa, gently toast the star anise in a small deep fryer to expel their oil.

15. Transfer the diced veggies, peppers, bread, cloves, almonds, walnuts, smoked paprika, cayenne pepper, balsamic vinegar, and sherry vinegar to a food processor till a crunchy paste with the texture of pesto forms.

16. Heat the oven to 200°C for the chicken breasts.

17. Sprinkle the olive oil over the chicken breasts on a sheet and sprinkle with salt.

18. Cook the chicken breasts for 3 minutes on each side in a warm deep fryer.

19. Roast for thirty minutes cut side down, with the tarragon and garlic.

20. Offer the marinated chicken thighs with romesco sauces, smashed almonds, and a squeeze of lemon juice on a base of romesco marinade.

3.9 Spicy Spanish Meatballs

Cooking Time: 35 minutes

Serving Size: 4

Ingredients:

Spanish Meatballs

- 2 ½ teaspoon smoked paprika
- ¼ cup olive oil
- 2 clove garlic
- 1 egg yolk
- 2 tablespoon milk
- 500 grams beef
- ½ cup breadcrumbs

Smoked Paprika Tomato Sauce

- ½ teaspoon smoked paprika
- 500 grams tomatoes
- 3 cloves garlic
- 1 bay leaf
- 1 onion
- 1 tablespoon olive oil

Method:

10. Soak the breadcrumbs in dairy for five minutes before pressing out any remaining water.
11. Add salt and pepper to taste.
12. Make 12 balls out of the flour mix and place them on a table to work with.
13. In a large skillet, heat the oil over medium heat.
14. Heat the meatballs for four minutes, rotating once or until golden brown.

15. Heat for about four minutes with the spray of excess oil, onions, ginger, and bay leaf.
16. Wait for another minute till the paprika is aromatic.
17. Transfer the meatballs to the bowl after stirring in the tomatoes.
18. Transfer to a serving bowl and serve right away.

3.10 Spanish One-Pan Chicken with Chorizo and Bell Peppers

Cooking Time: 1 hour

Serving Size: 5

Ingredients:

For Chicken

- 3 tablespoon tomato paste
- 3 cups chicken broth
- 2 garlic cloves
- 1 large ripe tomato
- 1 green bell pepper
- 1 red onion
- 1 ½ cup rice
- Olive oil
- 6 oz. Chorizo sausage
- 4 chicken drumsticks
- 4 chicken thighs

For Spice Rub

- 1 teaspoon black pepper
- ½ teaspoon cayenne pepper
- 1 teaspoon garlic powder
- 1 teaspoon salt
- 1 tablespoon smoked paprika

Method:
1. Wash the rice in water for a few minutes.
2. Enable the rice to soak for fifteen minutes after covering it with water.
3. Combine the ingredients, salt, and pepper in a small cup.
4. Season the chicken with salt and pepper.
5. Season the chicken with the spice rub after patting it dry.
6. Both sides of the chicken should be browned.
7. Add 1 tablespoon of additional olive oil, heat until glistening but not burning over medium-high heat.
8. Cook the chorizo and veggies together.
9. Prepare the chicken.
10. Combine the sliced tomatoes, tomato sauce, and chicken stock in a large mixing bowl.
11. Cook the rice in the same pot as the chicken.
12. Allow the chicken and rice to rest in the pan for a few minutes.
13. Remove the pan from the heat but keep it covered and unhindered for another ten minutes. Serve immediately.

3.11 Sizzling Spanish Garlic Prawns

Cooking Time: 13 minutes

Serving Size: 6

Ingredients:
- 6 garlic cloves
- 6 tablespoons dry sherry
- 1 teaspoon chili flakes
- 4 tablespoons olive oil
- 3 tablespoons parsley
- 900g raw king prawns

Method:
6. Preheat the oven to 220 degrees Celsius.
7. Simply cut the prawns lengthwise but not all the way through it and cut the vein to flap the shrimp.
8. Use 6 small oven tray dishes or one big one to separate the shrimp, garlic, chili or pimento, brandy, and balsamic vinegar.
9. Cook for 12 to 15 minutes until it is red and piping hot, based on the pan or pots' size.
10. Serve with toasted bread and citrus wedges, garnished with parsley.

3.12 Super Tasty Spanish Roast Chicken

Cooking Time: 1 hour 40 minutes

Serving Size: 8

Ingredients:

- Olive oil
- 2 cloves garlic
- Freshly ground black pepper
- 300g Iberico chorizo sausage
- 2kg chicken
- Sea salt
- 1.6kg potatoes
- 1 handful parsley
- 4 lemons

Method:

7. Heat your oven to 220°C, and put your vegetables in a large pan of boiling water containing two lemons and simmer for five minutes.
8. Take the leaves from the tarragon stalks and set them aside.
9. Fill the meat with the tarragon stalks and warm lemons.
10. Position the potato in the center of the baking parchment, then the poultry on top and the pancetta on top of that.
11. Whereas the chicken and vegetables are frying, make the gremolata, as the Italians name it.
12. Chop the poultry and serve with the potatoes on eight plates.

3.13 Spanish Mixed Green Salad

Cooking Time: 10 minutes

Serving Size: 4

Ingredients:

- ½ Spanish onion
- 10 -12 green olives
- 2 cups Boston lettuce
- 2 tomatoes
- 1 cup baby spinach
- 2 cups romaine lettuce

Dressing

- 3 tablespoons olive oil
- Sea salt and black pepper
- 1 tablespoon lemon juice

Method:

3. Combine all of the dressing components in a mixing bowl and whisk until thoroughly combined.
4. Toss with salad well before eating.

3.14 Spanish-Inspired Tomato Salad

Cooking Time: 40 minutes

Serving Size: 8

Ingredients:

- 16 caper berries
- 6 anchovy fillets
- 3 pounds tomatoes
- 1 cup parsley
- ½ teaspoon sugar
- ¼ teaspoon salt
- 1/3 cup olive oil
- 3 tablespoons sherry vinegar
- 1 teaspoon pepper
- 1 teaspoon paprika
- 1 cup fresh breadcrumbs
- 5 cloves garlic

Method:

8. In a large saucepan, warm 1/3 cup oil over moderate flame.
9. Cook, occasionally stirring, for about 20 seconds, just until the citrus is spicy and piping hot but not crispy.
10. In the same pan, heat and cook 2 tablespoons of oil over moderate flame.
11. Cook, constantly stirring, until the breadcrumbs are crisp and lightly browned, about five minutes.
12. In a mixing bowl, combine the garlic-paprika oil, mustard, spice, cinnamon, and salt.
13. Gently whisk in the onions, tarragon, caper fruit, and minced anchovies.

14. Serve the tomato salad on a large plate with the fried cornmeal on top.

Chapter 4: Tapas Dinner and Desserts

4.1 Spanish Rice Dinner

Cooking Time: 20 minutes
Serving Size: 4

Ingredients:

- ⅛ teaspoon pepper
- ⅛ teaspoon hot pepper sauce
- ½ teaspoon ground mustard
- ¼ teaspoon garlic powder
- 1 teaspoon salt
- 1 teaspoon Worcestershire sauce
- 1 tablespoon onion
- 1 tablespoon sugar
- 1 can stewed tomatoes
- 1 can green beans
- 1-½ cups cooked rice
- 1 pound ground beef

Method:

5. Steam beef when no pinker in a large frying pan; clean.
6. Add the rest of the ingredients and stir to combine.
7. Raise the temperature to be high and bring the mixture to a boil.

8. Reduce to a low heat environment, cover, and cook for 5-10 minutes, or until thoroughly cooked.

4.2 Shrimp and Chorizo Tapas

Cooking Time: 43 minutes
Serving Size: 8

Ingredients:
- 2 tablespoons parsley leaves
- Crusty bread, for serving
- 1½ pounds raw shrimp
- 3 tablespoons lemon juice
- 1 tablespoon Spanish olive oil
- 2 teaspoons salt
- 1 teaspoon black pepper
- ½ cup dry sherry
- 1 tablespoon Spanish paprika
- 1½ cups onion
- 1 tablespoon garlic
- 1 pound chorizo

Method:
1. 1 tablespoon olive oil, heated in a big skillet or cazuela, simmer the diced chorizo.
2. Cook, occasionally stirring, until the onion is caramelized around the outside.
3. Cook, constantly stirring, for two minutes after adding the garlic.
4. Cook for two minutes after adding ¼ cup of wine.

5. Cook for about 5-6 minutes after adding the shrimp, parmesan, 1 teaspoon salt, and 2 teaspoons black pepper.
6. Remove the pan from the heat and mix in the existing ¼ cup wine, ¼ cup balsamic vinegar, lime juice, tarragon, and the additional salt and pepper.

4.3 Tapas Style Garlic Mushrooms

Cooking Time: 10 minutes

Serving Size: 4

Ingredients:
- 1 tablespoon lemon juice
- 2 tablespoons fresh parsley
- Salt to taste
- ½ cup white wine
- 4 garlic cloves
- 2 pounds mushrooms
- 2 tablespoons olive oil

Method:
6. In a large skillet over medium heat, add the oil over moderate flame.
7. Cook the mushroom for five minutes, periodically tossing the pot.
8. Heat, flipping the pan often, for another 1-2 minutes or until crispy, adding the garlic, cayenne pepper, salt, and pepper.
9. Toss in the tarragon to mix everything.
10. Aioli and lime wedges should be served alongside the mushrooms.

4.4 Spicy Shrimp Tapas

Cooking Time: 30 minutes

Serving Size: 4

Ingredients:

- Zest of 1 lime
- Some herbs for garnish
- 2 tablespoon of olive oil
- 1 pinch of salt
- 1 tablespoon of fennel seeds
- 1 piece of fresh ginger
- 16 raw shrimp
- 1 large clove of garlic
- 1 tablespoon Sichuan pepper
- 1 mango

Method:

1. Remove the core from the fruit and cut it into 16 thin pieces.
2. Just retain the tail of the shrimp after shelling it.
3. Heat the oil, peppers, and tarragon in a medium saucepan until fragrant.
4. After that, insert the shrimp and a half-cut garlic clove.
5. Brown, occasionally stirring, for ten minutes.
6. Once the shrimp is finished, mix in the fresh ginger and salt for two minutes, then set aside to cool.
7. Then use a toothpick, pick up seafood and a fruit cube, continue with the remaining shrimp.

8. On a platter, arrange them in a row.
9. Garnish with a few new herbs and lemon zest.

4.5 Fruity Spanish Tapas

Cooking Time: 30 minutes
Serving Size: 4

Ingredients:
- 50g vegetarian manchego
- 1 tablespoon chives
- 1 tablespoon garlic oil
- 1 Pink Lady apple
- ¼ ciabatta

Method:
8. Trim the edges of the ciabatta blocks, so they sit flat on a surface.
9. Heat a baking tray to a high temperature.
10. Grill the ciabatta pieces for 2-3 minutes, rotating once, until finely charred all over.
11. Remove the board from the oven and place it on top of it.
12. Heat for 2-3 minutes, rotating halfway, till the apple slices are slightly charred.
13. To combine, place two slices of fruit, a cheese slice, and a sprinkling of chives on each cube of bread.
14. Serve after securing with a toothpick.

4.6 Spanish Tapas-Inspired Mussels

Cooking Time: 40 minutes

Serving Size: 2

Ingredients:

- ¼ cup dry sherry
- 2 pounds mussels
- Pinch of saffron
- ½ cup vegetable broth
- 2 teaspoons olive oil
- 2 teaspoons fresh oregano
- ½ teaspoon pepper
- 1 8-ounce can chickpeas
- 2 cloves garlic
- 1 4-ounce jar pimientos
- 1 small onion
- 8 cherry tomatoes

Method:

11. In a medium skillet, heat the oil over moderate flame.
12. Combine the chickpeas, onions, ginger, garlic, and pimentos in a large mixing bowl.
13. Process until tender, five to six minutes, stirring constantly.
14. Add oregano, cinnamon, and saffron and stir to combine.
15. Cook for about thirty seconds, stirring constantly.

16. Stir in the broth and red wine, scraping up any browned bits from the bottom of the pan.
17. Bring the liquid to a low boil, then reduce to low heat.
18. Stir in the mussels. Reduce the heat to a low temperature and keep it there.
19. Cover, lower heat and cook for five to six minutes, or until mussels open.
20. When serving, stir in the mussels and remove any that haven't opened.

4.7 Spanish-Style Chicken with Mushrooms

Cooking Time: 55 minutes

Serving Size: 4

Ingredients:

- 1½ cups chicken stock
- Fresh parsley to serve
- 4 cloves garlic
- 2 teaspoons Spanish paprika
- 4 chicken thighs
- 1 tablespoon thyme leaves
- 1 yellow onion
- 1 pound button mushrooms
- 2/3 cup dry white wine
- 2 tablespoons olive oil
- Salt and pepper

Method:

1. Dress the chicken breasts with salts and dried basil before cooking.
2. Steam the olive oil in a large cast-iron pan or grill over moderate flame.
3. On both ends, grill the chicken thighs uniformly.
4. Transfer the pan to the heat and add the vegetables, cooking for an additional five minutes.
5. Shift the oven temperature until the wine has decreased.
6. Stir together the carrots, ginger, paprika, and a pinch of salt.
7. Continue to sauté for another minute.
8. Decrease to a moderate heat area.
9. Transfer the chicken thighs to the pan with the chicken broth, then cover with a cap.
10. Serve immediately with clean parsley on top.

4.8 Avocado and Tuna Tapas

Cooking Time: 20 minutes

Serving Size: 4

Ingredients:

- 1 pinch garlic salt
- 2 ripe avocados
- 1 dash balsamic vinegar
- Black pepper to taste
- 3 green onions
- ½ red bell pepper
- 1 tablespoon mayonnaise

- 1 can solid white tuna

Method:

4. In a mixing bowl, combine the tuna, mayo, spring onions, bell pepper, and maple syrup.

5. Dress with peppers and garlic salt, then stuff the tuna combination into the avocado halves.

6. Before eating, garnish with the reserved spring onions and a pinch of smoked paprika.

4.9 Fish Tapas

Cooking Time: 40 minutes

Serving Size: 4

Ingredients:

- 40g butter
- 500ml salt
- 110g peas
- 40g flour
- 1 carrot
- 1 bay leaf
- 200g flour
- 12 mussels
- 1 onion
- 100ml olive oil
- Salt
- 200g cod
- 3 tablespoons water

- 1 egg

Method:

11. Combine the flour, oil, yolk, liquid, and a bit of salt to make a pastry.
12. In boiled water, cook fish and mussels with cabbage, carrot, and lemon zest.
13. Strip the mussels from their skins until cooked and cut finely.
14. Remove some bones from the fish and chop it up.
15. In boiled water, prepare the vegetable peas.
16. Create a thick white liquid with the oil in a frying pan.
17. Combine the diced fish, mussels, and peas in a large mixing bowl.
18. Seal the sides of the pastry by folding it over.
19. Keep 10 to 15 minutes in a deep fryer.
20. Serve with fried tarragon on the side.

4.10 Spanish Rice Skillet Meal

Cooking Time: 28 minutes

Serving Size: 4

Ingredients:

- 1 can tomatoes
- 1 can tomatoes with green chilies
- ⅛ teaspoon black pepper
- ½ cup water
- ½ teaspoon cumin
- ¼ teaspoon salt
- ¾ pound ground beef
- ¼ teaspoon oregano
- ½ teaspoon chili powder
- 2 tablespoons olive oil
- 1 clove garlic
- ¾ cup uncooked white rice
- ½ medium onion

Method:

9. In a large frying pan, brown the ground beef, stirring constantly.
10. Drain the water and set it aside.
11. On moderate flame, drizzle vegetable oil into the pan.
12. Sauté onions for three minutes, or until soft.
13. Mix in the garlic and grain until the rice is finely browned.

14. Combine the ground beef, oregano, chili powder, smoked paprika, salt, black pepper, and tomatoes in a large mixing bowl.

15. Get the water to a boil.

16. Reduce to medium heat, cover, and cook for 20 minutes, or till all liquid has been absorbed.

4.11 Champinones Spanish Garlic Mushrooms

Cooking Time: 10 minutes

Serving Size: 4

Ingredients:

- ½ teaspoon chili flakes
- 1 tablespoon flat-leaf parsley
- ¼ teaspoon Spanish paprika
- Ground pepper and sea salt
- 10 large button mushrooms
- 1 tablespoon lemon juice
- 2 tablespoons dry sherry
- 3 tablespoons olive oil
- 5 cloves garlic

Method:

6. The mushrooms should be quartered, the parsley should be chopped, and the garlic should be crushed.

7. Add the olive oil and simmer the mushrooms for several moments over moderate flame.

8. Then, with the exception of the parsley, combine the rest of the ingredients.

9. Cook for another five minutes, stirring occasionally.
10. Then take the pan from the heat and whisk in the grated parmesan.

4.12 Catalan Fig Tapas

Cooking Time: 15 minutes

Serving Size: 4

Ingredients:
- 4 slices Jamon
- 100g manchego cheese
- 8 slices of wood-fired bread
- 1 garlic clove
- 8 figs
- 6 thyme sprigs
- ¼ cup olive oil

Method:
7. Preheat a chargrill or a barbecue to high temperature.
8. Toss the doubled figs with canola oil, minced parsley, and a bit of salt in a mixing cup.
9. Roast the figs for two minutes on each hand or until they are soft and caramelized.
10. Rub the bread with excess oil in both directions and grill for 1-two minutes on either side until it's crispy and charred.
11. The cut surface of the garlic clove should be rubbed on one side of each piece.
12. Place two fig pieces on each chargrilled loaf piece.

13. Serve hot, topped with Jamun and grilled manchego.

4.13 Quick and Easy Paella

Cooking Time: 1 hour 10 minutes
Serving Size: 6

Ingredients:
Saffron Broth
- ½ teaspoon saffron threads
- 2 ¼ cups chicken broth
- 2 teaspoons olive oil
- 1 pound jumbo shrimp

Paella
- 1 teaspoon paprika
- 1 pinch cayenne pepper
- 1 red bell pepper
- Salt to taste
- 1 ⅓ cups Arborio rice
- ½ cup green peas
- 1 tablespoon olive oil
- ½ yellow onion
- 2 cloves garlic
- 8 ounces chorizo sausage

Method:
10. In a pan over medium heat, steam, and mix preserved shrimp shells and two teaspoons canola oil.

11. Saffron should be stirred into the shells, and chicken broth should be added.
12. Preheat the oven to 425 degrees Fahrenheit.
13. In a large oven-safe skillet, heat one tablespoon of olive oil on medium-high heat. In a hot skillet, cook chorizo strips.
14. Continue cooking the garlic into the chorizo combination until moist.
15. Over the rice, place the seafood in a thin layer.
16. Sprinkle with salt, parmesan, and cayenne pepper, and place pepper slices around as well as between shrimp.
17. Cook the rice paste for 20 minutes in a preheated oven.
18. Cook, often stirring, until the rice is soft, the liquid has been absorbed, and the rice has caramelized.

Chapter 5: Classic Spanish Dishes

5.1 Spanish Style Albondigas

Cooking Time: 2 hours 20 minutes
Serving Size: 4

Ingredients:
- 1 can plum tomatoes
- 2 tablespoons olive oil
- 1 cup white wine
- 2 tablespoons tomato puree
- ¼ teaspoon coriander
- 2 grinds black pepper
- ⅔ pound beef
- 1 ½ teaspoons basil
- 1 ½ teaspoons oregano
- ⅓ pound pork
- 2 tablespoons celery
- 1 clove garlic
- 2 tablespoons carrot
- 3 ½ ounces pancetta
- 3 tablespoons onion
- 3 ½ ounces white bread crumbs
- 2 tablespoons olive oil
- 2 tablespoons red bell pepper
- 2 dashes Worcestershire sauce

- Salt and pepper
- 2 tablespoons green onion
- 1 tablespoon fresh parsley
- 1 clove garlic
- 2 tablespoons fresh oregano

Method:

9. In a mixing bowl, combine ground beef, pork belly, spring onions, oregano, tarragon, garlic, Balsamic vinegar, salt, and black pepper.
10. Slowly stir in the breadcrumbs until the meat mixture reaches the perfect consistency.
11. Freezer meatballs for at least 30 minutes after wrapping them in cling film.
12. In a big saucepan, steam 2 tablespoons olive oil on medium-high heat.
13. In a hot skillet, continue cooking pancetta until it is golden brown, about four minutes. Toss in the vegetables and seasoning.
14. In a wide skillet, steam 2 tablespoons of oil over medium heat.
15. 6 to 10 minutes, continue cooking meatballs in hot oil quantities until uniformly browned and heated through.
16. Transfer the meatballs softly into the boiling sauce and cook together until the meatballs are thoroughly cooked.

5.2 Mediterranean Basa Stew & Sunny Aioli

Cooking Time: 1 hour

Serving Size: 2

Ingredients:

- 1 white wine vinegar
- 1 carrot
- 1 garlic clove
- 1 tomato paste
- 2 ciabatta rolls
- 1 mayonnaise
- 1 garlic clove
- 1 vegetable stock
- 1 brown onion
- 1 teaspoon ground turmeric
- 5g parsley
- 2 x 100g basa fillets
- 1-star anise
- 1 bag of pitted black olives

Method:

10. Preheat the oven to 220 degrees Celsius.
11. Use a drizzle of canola oil, heat a big, wide-based pan.
12. Insert the chopped onion, sliced carrot, and a quarter of the garlic once the pan is warmed.
13. Heat for 6-8 minutes, just until the onions are soft and transparent, after adding the star anise.

14. Whisk together the mayo, the leftover minced garlic, the red wine vinegar, and add salt and pepper.
15. Place the ciabatta rolls on a baking sheet and bake them for 8-10 minutes.
16. Warm a drizzle of olive oil in a separate wide broad pan over medium temperature.
17. When the pan is warmed, skin-side up, add the sea bass, and boil for four minutes.
18. With the warm ciabatta on the side, place the grilled sea bass over the soup.

5.3 Mediterranean Olive Toss

Cooking Time: 45 minutes

Serving Size: 8

Ingredients:
- 2 cups spinach leaves
- ½ cup feta cheese
- 7 pickled red peppers
- ¼ cup Kalamata olives
- 1 package penne pasta
- 4 large cloves of garlic
- 1 (8 ounces) jar artichoke
- ⅓ cup olive oil

Method:
7. Fill a large pot halfway with liquid and bring to the boil, lightly toasted.
8. Return to a boil after adding the penne.
9. Heat pasta for ten minutes, covered, then rinse.

10. In a large skillet over medium heat, heat the olive oil on moderate heat and cook and mix garlic once aromatic, around 30 seconds.

11. 5 minutes after adding the pine nuts, tomatoes, and artichokes to the skillet, stir to combine flavors.

12. Remove from the heat and stir in the penne pasta until well combined; toss the pasta mixture gently with the feta cheese.

5.4 Spanish Orange & Olive Salad

Cooking Time: 20 minutes

Serving Size: 4

Ingredients:

For the Softened Leeks

- ¼ teaspoon kosher salt
- 1 tablespoon water
- 1 tablespoon white wine vinegar
- 1 small leek

For the Orange & Olive Salad

- Squeeze lemon juice
- ¼ cup Marcona almonds
- Sprinkle flaky sea salt
- Sprinkle Sumac
- 6 oranges
- 4 teaspoon leek vinegar marinade
- 1 tablespoon olive oil
- 3 tablespoon softened leeks

- ⅓ cup halved olives

Method:

11. To begin, prepare and marinate the leeks.

12. Cut the white color green pieces into rounds with a thin knife.

13. 1 tablespoon balsamic vinegar syrup, sea salt, and 1 tablespoon water are combined with the leeks.

14. Allow fifteen minutes for the leeks to caramelize, tossing periodically.

15. Cut the oranges into circles after segmenting them.

16. Cast aside half of the olives.

17. In a medium mixing bowl, combine the bananas, olives, and 3 tablespoons of the brined leeks.

18. Toss in 4 teaspoons of the leek marinade and 4 teaspoons of olive oil in a mixing bowl softly.

19. Add a pinch of flaky sea salt, sumac, a splash of lime juice, and nuts to the salad.

20. Serve directly after garnishing.

5.5 Pisto (Spanish Vegetable Stew)

Cooking Time: 1 hour 20 minutes
Serving Size: 8

Ingredients:
- 1 teaspoon honey
- 2 medium zucchini
- 1.5 cans tomatoes
- 1.5 teaspoons salt
- 1 green bell pepper
- 2 garlic cloves
- 1 large eggplant
- ½ long red chili
- 1 red bell pepper
- Good quality olive oil
- 1 large onion
- ½ teaspoon salt

Method:

10. Spray the eggplant with salts and slice it into pieces.
11. Allow for 15-20 minutes of rest time.
12. In a big, roasting pan, heat four tablespoons of canola oil over moderate flame.
13. Combine the onions, chili, and diced beans in a large mixing bowl. Cook for 12-14 minutes over moderate flame.
14. Fry for 4-5 minutes, mixing halfway through, until the eggplant is golden brown.

15. Remove the eggplant from the pan and drizzle with a little more canola oil.
16. Cook for another 4-5 minutes after adding the zucchini.
17. Ultimately, mix in the pre-fried zucchini and eggplant to the tomatoes concentrate in the pot.
18. Cover and cook for 25 minutes over a moderate flame with a seal.

5.6 Mediterranean Skillet Chicken with Bulgur Paella, Carrots

Cooking Time: 50 minutes

Serving Size: 4

Ingredients:

Lemon Yogurt Sauce

- Pinch of cayenne pepper
- Kosher salt
- Zest and juice of 1 lemon
- 2 tablespoons curly parsley
- 1½ cups plain yogurt

For the Chicken

- ½ cup golden raisins
- ½ cup curly parsley sprigs
- 2 cups safflower oil
- ½ cup whole blanched almonds
- 6 chicken thighs
- 2 bay leaves

- 1½ cups basmati rice
- 4 whole cloves
- 2 cinnamon sticks
- 3 cups chicken stock
- 5 cardamom pods
- 6 chicken drumsticks
- 2 tablespoons tomato paste
- 3 strips orange zest
- Kosher salt and pepper
- ½ teaspoon turmeric
- 2 tomatoes
- 2 tablespoons olive oil
- 1 teaspoon cumin
- 1 teaspoon coriander
- 1 large onion
- 2 teaspoons fresh ginger
- ½ cup grated carrot
- 3 cloves garlic

Method:

9. Combine yogurt, lime juice and zest, tarragon, and smoked paprika in a medium mixing cup.
10. Put aside after seasoning with salt.
11. Preheat the oven to 375 degrees Fahrenheit.
12. Season the chicken with salt and pepper before serving.
13. Reduce the heat to medium-low and add the spices.

14. Place them skin-side up golden brown chicken in the boiling liquid and bake for 25 minutes.

15. Take the rice to a boil in a saucepan with the stored liquid ingredients over moderate flame.

16. Stir in the rice, cover, and cook on low heat until the rice is tender, about 20 minutes.

5.7 Rustic Spanish Chicken Casserole

Cooking Time: 1 hour 20 minutes
Serving Size: 6

Ingredients:

- ½ teaspoon cayenne pepper
- 1 cup basil leaves
- 1 teaspoon dried oregano
- ½ teaspoon smoked paprika
- 1 cup stuffed pimento olives
- 1 carrot, diced
- 1 red bell pepper
- 2 tablespoon tomato paste
- 1 can cannellini beans
- ½ cup chicken stock
- 1 tablespoon olive oil
- 8 chicken thigh cutlets
- 2 cans tomatoes
- 3 garlic cloves
- 1 white onion

Method:

9. Preheat the oven to 180 degrees Celsius.
10. In a huge slow cooker, heat the oil over moderate flame.
11. For a few minutes, sauté the cloves and vegetables until they are translucent.

12. Cook for a few minutes after adding the chicken thighs.
13. With the exception of the basil leaves, combine all of the remaining ingredients in a mixing bowl.
14. 5 minutes on top of the burner, heat until softly bubbling.
15. Preheat the oven to 350°F and bake for 45 minutes on average.
16. Serve with carrots or cabbage rice.

5.8 Mediterranean Seafood Stew

Cooking Time: 45 minutes

Serving Size: 6

Ingredients:

- 3 tablespoon toasted pine nuts
- Crusty Italian bread
- 2 lb. skinless sea bass fillet
- ½ cup fresh parsley leaves
- Olive oil
- ¼ cup golden raisins
- 2 tablespoon capers
- 1 large yellow onion
- 1 28-oz. can plum tomatoes
- 3 cups vegetable broth
- Pinch red pepper flakes
- ¾ cup dry white wine
- 2 celery ribs

- 4 large garlic cloves
- ½ teaspoon dried thyme
- Salt and pepper

Method:
10. 1 tablespoon olive oil, heated over moderate flame.
11. Add the onions, fennel, and a pinch of salt and pepper to taste.
12. Cook for a few minutes until the thyme, red pepper flakes, and cloves are aromatic.
13. Decrease the fluid by about ½ percent by getting it to a simmer.
14. Combine the peppers, vegetable broth, pecans, and chives in a large mixing bowl.
15. Cook for 15-20 minutes over a moderate flame, stirring periodically until the flavors have melded.
16. Place the fish parts in the liquid ingredients and gently stir them all together. Cover the Dutch oven and turn off the heat.
17. Mix in the chopped parsley last.
18. Fill serving bowls halfway with the spicy fish stew.

5.9 Saucy Spanish Chicken with Green Olives

Cooking Time: 150 minutes

Serving Size: 8

Ingredients:
- ¼ cup sherry

- 1 tablespoon cornstarch
- 2 teaspoon dried thyme
- 1 teaspoon cumin and paprika
- 8 chicken drumsticks
- 1 small red onion
- 2 large garlic cloves
- 1 cup green olives
- 389ml can tomato sauce

Method:

8. Remove the skin from the chicken and remove any excess fat.
9. Pour the sauce in. Quantify out the artichokes, then cut them up and throw them in.
10. Combine the onion, ginger, thyme, smoked paprika, and tarragon in a mixing bowl.
11. Place the chicken in the paste to coat it, then turn it bone-side out. Push your way into the liquid.
12. Cook for six hours on medium or 2½ to 3 hours on average, or until chicken reaches 165°F.
13. Combine cornstarch and a few tablespoons of water in a mixing bowl and whisk until smooth.
14. Stir frequently in the sauce until it thickens, around five minutes. Chicken should be served over rice.

5.10 Summer Spanish Salad

Cooking Time: 10 minutes

Serving Size: 2

Ingredients:

- 3 tablespoons olive oil
- 2 tablespoon red wine vinegar
- A pinch of cumin
- ½ teaspoon salt
- 2 large tomatoes
- 1 large green pepper
- 2 cloves garlic minced
- 1 medium onion
- 1 large cucumber

Method:

7. Dip the onions in water after cutting them into small cubes.
8. Position the tomatoes, celery, and peppers in a cup and chop them up.
9. Drain the vegetables and combine them with the remaining ingredients.
10. In a separate small cup, combine the remaining olive oil, vinegar, and salt, then stir in the garlic paste.
11. Toss the salad with the dressing and toss well.
12. Cover and store in the refrigerator.

5.11 Rice Spanish Vegetables Recipe

Cooking Time: 45 minutes

Serving Size: 8

Ingredients:

- ½ teaspoon salt
- Chopped cilantro
- 2 teaspoons cumin
- 1 teaspoon chili powder
- ¾ cup corn kernels
- ½ cup peas
- 3 tablespoons olive oil
- 1 cup tomatoes
- 2 2/3 cups vegetable broth
- 1 small onion
- 1½ cups white rice
- 1 tablespoon tomato paste
- 1 large carrot
- 3 cloves garlic
- 1 medium green pepper

Method:

1. In a medium saucepan, heat the oil on moderate flame.
2. Add the onion, garlic, and carrots to the hot oil.
3. Cook for an additional minute, just until the vegetables have softened.

4. Cook for thirty seconds, just until the garlic is fragrant. Toss in the rice.
5. Mix in the chopped tomatoes, then insert the tomatoes, stock, corn, peas, cumin, chili powder, and salt to taste.
6. Remove the rice from the heat and set it aside for ten minutes, covered.
7. Toss the rice with a spoon to fluff it up.
8. Taste and sprinkle with more salt if necessary, then top with coriander.

5.12 Mediterranean Wrap

Cooking Time: 10 minutes

Serving Size: 1

Ingredients:

- 2 tablespoons basil pesto
- 1-2 tablespoons feta cheese
- ¼ cup rotisserie chicken
- 3 tablespoons tomatoes
- 1 cow cheese wedge
- ½ cup greens lettuce
- 1 tortilla wrap

Method:

7. Place the tortilla on a flat surface and scatter the Laughing Cow cheesy wedge down the middle.
8. Insert the mixed greens just to the side of the cheese.
9. Cover with the meat, sun-dried vegetables, and pesto, spooned on top and softly spread.
10. Over the risotto, break the gruyere cheese.
11. Fold the upper part of the tortilla inwards somewhat, then roll it up tightly.
12. Break the wrap in half with a sharp knife and eat right away!

5.13 Easy Tomato Gazpacho Recipe

Cooking Time: 15 minutes

Serving Size: 6

Ingredients:

- A small handful of mint leaves
- Small cilantro leaves
- 5 slices stale artisan bread
- 1 teaspoon cayenne pepper
- Pinch sugar
- Water
- Salt and pepper
- ½ teaspoon cumin
- 5 large ripe tomatoes
- Olive oil
- 2 tablespoon sherry vinegar
- ½ English cucumber
- 2 green onions
- 2 garlic cloves
- 1 green pepper
- 1 celery stalk

Method:

10. In a pan, combine the bread slices and ½ cup of water.
11. Remove the tops of the tomatoes.

12. Combine the tomatoes, carrots, fennel, green beans, fresh basil, and garlic in a big blender or food processor.

13. Place the soaking bread on top.

14. Pour ½ cup olive oil and sherry wine into a mixing bowl.

15. If the gazpacho is too thick, add more water and mix again until consistency is right.

16. Fill a glass beaker or wide canning jar with the mixture.

17. Cover tightly with plastic wrap and place in the refrigerator to cool.

18. Offer the gazpacho a short swirl before transferring it to serving bowls or small glasses.

5.14 Spanish Tuna and Potato Salad Recipe

Cooking Time: 24 minutes

Serving Size: 8

Ingredients:

- 3 tablespoon white wine vinegar
- 6 oz. spring greens
- ½ teaspoon red pepper flakes
- ⅓ cup Greek olive oil
- 1 teaspoon smoked paprika
- ¾ teaspoon cumin
- 3 large garlic cloves
- Salt and pepper
- 12 oz. fingerling potatoes

- ⅓ cup pearl red onions
- 15 oz. can quality tuna
- 6 oz. small tomatoes
- 10 oz. French green beans

Method:

11. Fill a big pot halfway with water and add the fingerling vegetables.

12. Cook for ten minutes at a low temperature.

13. Fill a wide bowl halfway with ice water and place it next to the pot.

14. Green beans should be added to the hot water in the same frying pan.

15. Cook for about four minutes.

16. Wash the green beans and instantly placed them in the ice water bowl.

17. Green beans, peppers, tomatoes, fish, and garlic are added to the pot.

18. Add Salt, powder, parmesan, cumin, and ground red pepper to taste.

19. Toss all together gently to ensure that all of the components are properly coated.

20. Taste and change seasoning, if necessary, by adding more smoked paprika, cilantro, or smashed red pepper.

5.15 Easy Seafood Paella Recipe

Cooking Time: 1 hour

Serving Size: 6

Ingredients:

- 1 lb. prawns
- ¼ cup fresh parsley
- 2 large Roma tomatoes
- 6 oz. French green beans
- 4 small lobster tails
- ½ teaspoon chili pepper flakes
- Salt
- Water
- 1 teaspoon Spanish paprika
- 1 teaspoon cayenne pepper
- 3 tablespoon olive oil
- 4 garlic cloves
- 2 large pinches of saffron
- 2 cups Spanish rice
- 1 large yellow onion

Method:

10. Take 3 cups of water to a gentle simmer in a big saucepan.

11. Tongs are used to cut the lobster tails.

12. After 2 minutes of sautéing the onions, add the garlic and cook for another 3 minutes, stirring frequently.

13. Combine the saffron, dripping water, paprika, smoked paprika, Aleppo paprika, and salt in a mixing bowl.

14. Combine the tomato slices and green beans in a mixing bowl.

15. Cook for an additional ten minutes, just until the seafood changes color.

16. Add the cooked seafood chunks last.

17. Serve with rosemary as a garnish.

18. With your favorite white wine, eat the paella sweet.

5.16 One Pan Spanish Chicken and Rice Recipe with Chorizo

Cooking Time: 1 hour

Serving Size: 5

Ingredients:

For Chicken

- 3 tablespoon tomato paste
- 3 cups chicken broth
- 2 garlic cloves
- 1 large ripe tomato
- 1 ½ cup rice
- 1 large green bell pepper
- 1 medium red onion
- 4 chicken thighs
- Olive oil
- 6 oz. bulk chorizo sausage

- 4 chicken drumsticks

For Spice Rub

- 1 teaspoon black pepper
- ½ teaspoon cayenne pepper
- 1 teaspoon garlic powder
- 1 teaspoon salt
- 1 tablespoon smoked paprika

Method:

14. Soak the grain in water for a few minutes.
15. Position the rice in a bowl after thoroughly rinsing it.
16. Combine the ingredients, salt, and peppers in a small cup.
17. Dress the chicken with salt and pepper.
18. Both sides of the chicken should be browned.
19. Cautiously put the chicken in the pot and cook both sides thoroughly.
20. Transfer the chorizo to the same plate.
21. Combine the green beans, onions, and garlic in a large mixing bowl.
22. Cook for five minutes over a moderate flame, stirring frequently.
23. Combine the sliced tomatoes, tomato sauce, and chicken stock in a large mixing b
24. owl. Return the browned poultry to the bowl. Cook for 20 to 30 minutes at 350°F.
25. Cook the rice in the same pot as the chicken.

26. Allow the chicken and rice to rest in the pan for a few minutes.

5.17 20-Minute Couscous Recipe with Shrimp and Chorizo

Cooking Time: 25 minutes

Serving Size: 6

Ingredients:

- Boiling water
- 1 cup fresh parsley
- 1.5 lb. large shrimp
- 1 ¼ cup couscous
- 1 ¼ teaspoon ground cumin
- Salt
- 1 ¼ teaspoon turmeric
- 1 ¼ teaspoon paprika
- 6 oz. hard Spanish Chorizo
- 3 garlic cloves
- 2 jalapeno peppers
- 1 small yellow onion
- Extra virgin olive

Method:

11. Heat a small amount of vegetable oil in a large frying pan.
12. Heat the Chorizo sausage rolls until they are crisp.
13. Remove from the heat and clean on towels.

14. Add the garlic, onions, and habanero to the boiling pot and cook till the vegetables are transparent.
15. Now insert the seasoning and mix for a few seconds before adding the shrimp.
16. Heat the shrimp for approximately 3 minutes on moderate flame.
17. In the meantime, bring 2 ½ cups of water to a boil.
18. Transfer the couscous, little more vegetable oil, a pinch of salt, and the hot oil to the frying pan with the Chorizo.
19. Allow for five minutes of resting time. Remove the cover and add the fresh parsley.
20. Enjoy by moving to serve pots.

5.18 Gambas al Ajillo

Cooking Time: 20 minutes

Serving Size: 4

Ingredients:

- 2 tablespoons dry sherry
- 1 tablespoon Italian parsley
- 1 teaspoon hot smoked paprika
- ¼ cup extra-virgin olive oil
- 1 pound shrimp
- 4 cloves garlic

Method:

8. Finely cut garlic. Paprika and sea salt are used to season the shrimp. To coat, mix it.

9. In a pan, cook the garlic and oil on moderate flame.
10. Cook for about two minutes or until the garlic begins to turn translucent.
11. Increase the heat to the extreme and add the shrimp.
12. Toss and rotate the shrimp with tongs for around two minutes or until they start to curl but are still uncooked.
13. Pour the sherry in. Heat, constantly stirring, for 1 minute more, or till sauces come to boiling and shrimp is fried through.
14. Remove the pan from the heat. With a spoon, fold in the parsley.

5.19 Mediterranean-Style Steamed Clams Recipe

Cooking Time: 1 hour

Serving Size: 4

Ingredients:
- 1 green onion
- ⅓ cup parsley
- 1 ½ cup water
- 3 pounds littleneck clams
- Extra virgin olive oil
- ½ teaspoon red pepper flakes
- 1 cup dry white wine
- 1 yellow onion
- ½ teaspoon cumin

- ½ teaspoon smoked paprika
- ½ green pepper
- Salt and pepper
- 2 ripe tomatoes
- 4 garlic cloves minced
- ½ red pepper

Method:

14. Clams should be cleaned.
15. Put down the clams in the first container of cool simmering water for about 20 minutes.
16. To make the red wine soup, add all of the ingredients to a big mixing bowl.
17. ¼ cup olive oil, heated in a big Dutch oven over moderate flame.
18. Combine the onions, tomatoes, and garlic in a large mixing bowl.
19. Cook for five minutes after seasoning with kosher salt and black pepper.
20. Add the onions, smoked paprika, parmesan, and garlic powder, and stir to combine.
21. Combine the white wine and liquid in a mixing bowl.
22. Process for a few minutes, just until the tomato is slightly softened.
23. In a red wine sauce, heat the clams.
24. Reduce the heat to medium-low and add the clams.
25. Cook, covered until the remainder of the clams has opened.

26. Switch off the heat. Combine the spring onions and parsley in a mixing bowl.

5.20 Easy Spanish Tortilla Recipe

Cooking Time: 50 minutes

Serving Size: 4

Ingredients:
- 8 eggs, beaten
- Handful flat-leaf parsley
- 400g waxy potatoes
- 6 garlic cloves
- 4 tablespoon olive oil
- 25g butter
- 1 large white onion

To Serve
- 4 vine tomatoes
- Drizzle of olive oil
- 1 baguette

Method:
7. Preheat a large nonstick deep fryer to medium.
8. Steadily roast the onion in the butter and oil until it is tender. Slice the tomatoes in the meantime.
9. Add the potatoes to the skillet, wrap, and cook for another 15-20 minutes, occasionally mixing to ensure even cooking.
10. Add 2 garlic cloves crushed and mixed in, followed by pounded eggs.

11. Replace the lid on the pan and bake the tortilla on low heat.
12. When the tortilla is finished, move it to a plate and eat it warm or hot, with grated parmesan on top.

Chapter 6: Tapas Vegetarian Recipes

6.1 Spanish Vegetarian Stew

Cooking Time: 1 hour 20 minutes
Serving Size: 8

Ingredients:

- 1 teaspoon honey
- 2 small zucchini
- 1.5 cans tomatoes passata
- 1.5 teaspoons salt
- 1 green bell pepper
- 2 garlic cloves
- 1 large eggplant
- ½ long red chili
- 1 red bell pepper
- Good quality olive oil
- 1 large onion
- ½ teaspoon salt

Method:

10. Spray the eggplant with salts and slice it into pieces.
11. In a large frying pan, pour 4 tablespoons of vegetable oil.
12. Combine the onions, chili, and sliced peppers in a large mixing bowl.
13. Cook for ten minutes after adding the cloves and tomato.

14. Heat for 4-5 minutes, just until the eggplant is slightly golden brown.
15. Take the eggplant from the pan and drizzle with a little more coconut oil.
16. Heat, mixing a couple of times, for another 4-5 minutes with the zucchini.
17. Ultimately, mix in the pre-fried eggplant and sweet potato to the tomato mixture in the cup.
18. After frying, set aside for five minutes before serving.

6.2 Spanish Vegan Paella

Cooking Time: 45 minutes

Serving Size: 5

Ingredients:

- 2 sprigs of fresh thyme
- ¾ cup frozen peas
- 1 teaspoon sea salt
- Fresh cracked pepper
- 3 tablespoons olive oil
- 1 teaspoon smoked paprika
- ½ teaspoon sweet paprika
- 4 cups vegetable broth
- 1 large tomato
- 1 ½ cups Bomba Rice
- 1 red bell pepper
- 5 cloves garlic

- 1 medium onion
- 1 teaspoon saffron threads

Method:
11. In a small saucepan, insert vegetable broth.
12. In a 12-inch Paella Bowl, heat two tablespoons of oil and add the vegetables and spices.
13. Sauté until the vegetables are tender and golden brown.
14. Sauté for two minutes after adding the garlic.
15. Combine the onions, spicy paprika, and sweet paprika in a mixing bowl.
16. Cook for 1-2 minutes on high heat.
17. In the same pan, add the rice and the leftover 1 tablespoon of oil.
18. Put in the liquid slowly while adding the fresh thyme. Season with salt and pepper.
19. Reduce the heat to a low simmer.
20. Switch off the heat in the pan. Toss in the peas on top of the rice.

6.3 Tofu and Olive Tapas

Cooking Time: 43 minutes

Serving Size: 4

Ingredients:

For the Marinade

- ½ teaspoon black pepper
- ½ teaspoon chili flakes
- ½ teaspoon dried oregano
- ½ teaspoon salt
- 2 teaspoon paprika

For the Dish

- 50g Kalamata olives
- Small bunch of parsley
- 3 tablespoon vegetable stock
- 4 large plum tomatoes
- 4 tablespoon olive oil
- 1-star anise
- 3 tablespoon sherry
- ½ teaspoon chili flakes
- 3 cloves of garlic

Method:

9. Combine all of the components in a bowl or bag and stir well to combine the marinade.
10. Toss in the tofu and mix well. Cover and set aside for thirty minutes to marinate.
11. Cook the tofu parts in 2 tablespoons olive oil for 3-4 minutes, then set aside to keep warm.
12. In the cooking liquid, softly fry the garlic for 1-2 minutes.

13. Combine the chili flakes, chipotle powder, red wine, and vegetable stock in a large mixing bowl.
14. Cook, occasionally stirring, until the fluid has been reduced by half.
15. Medium heat for 2-3 minutes after adding the tofu, peppers, olives, and tarragon.
16. Serve with toasted bread right away.

6.4 Veggie Loaded Spanish Style Rice

Cooking Time: 45 minutes
Serving Size: 8

Ingredients:
- ½ teaspoon salt
- Chopped cilantro for garnish
- 2 teaspoons cumin
- 1 teaspoon chili powder
- ¾ cup corn kernels
- ½ cup frozen peas
- 1 cup tomatoes
- 2 2/3 cups vegetable broth
- 1½ cups white rice
- 1 tablespoon tomato paste
- 3 tablespoons olive oil
- 1 large carrot
- 3 cloves garlic
- 1 medium green pepper
- 1 small onion

Method:

8. In a medium saucepan, heat the oil over moderate flame.
9. Combine the onion, tomato, and carrot in a mixing bowl.
10. Cook for an additional minute or until the veggies have softened.

11. Cook for thirty seconds after adding the garlic.
12. Mix in the chopped tomatoes, then insert the tomatoes, stock, corn, peas, smoked paprika, chili powder, and salt to taste.
13. Toss the rice with a fork to fluff it up.
14. After tasting, add the coriander and serve.

6.5 Veggie Spanish-style Chorizo Omelets

Cooking Time: 55 minutes

Serving Size: 8

Ingredients:

For the Roasted Vegetables

- 2 tablespoon olive oil
- Salt and pepper to taste
- 2 medium potatoes
- ¾ teaspoon smoky BBQ seasoning
- 2 medium red onions
- 1 red pepper

For the Omelet

- 8 yolk eggs

For the Veggie Chorizo

- 1 teaspoon olive oil
- 8 shroom does

Method:

8. Heat the oven to 220 degrees Celsius.
9. Stir the chicken pieces, peppers, sliders, and onions chopped with the smoky spices and vegetable oil for the steamed veggies.
10. Fry the potato for 25-30 minutes, or till they have hardened.
11. Heat the chorizo-style shroomdogs over the last fifteen minutes of the veggies frying.
12. Remove the veggies from the oven until they are finished.
13. Slowly transfer the egg mixture into the pan, being careful not to disturb anything.
14. Season the eggs with salt and black pepper to taste, then uniformly distribute the leftover sausage strips and veggies on top.

6.6 Smoked Vegetarian Spanish Rice Recipe

Cooking Time: 45 minutes

Serving Size: 4

Ingredients:

- 1 coal
- Salt, to taste
- ½ teaspoon red chili powder
- ¼ cheddar cheese
- 1 cups basmati rice
- ¼ cup sweet corn
- ¼ cup green peas

- 2 tablespoons olive oil
- 3 tomatoes
- 2 stalks celery
- 1 onion
- 4 cloves garlic
- 1 green bell pepper
- 2 green chilies

Method:

9. In a large skillet, heat the oil over moderate heat and cook the garlic, onion, green pepper, diced peppers, and fennel until ready.
10. On low to moderate heat, sauté the vegetables and bell peppers until they are fully soft.
11. Add the onion, pepper, and chili powder once they have softened, and continue to cook until the vegetables are soft and tender.
12. Add the rice, beans, carrots, salt, and peppers, as well as two cups of water to the pot.
13. Turn the heat down and let the Spanish rice sit for around ten minutes after cooking.
14. A teaspoon of ghee or oil should be poured over the hot coal.
15. The rice will absorb the flavors of the smoked meat.
16. To mix all of the flavors and ingredients in the Spinach Rice, stir it thoroughly.

6.7 Tapas & Pinchos Vegetarian

Cooking Time: 30 minutes
Serving Size: 2

Ingredients:

Garlic Aioli Ingredients

- ½ cup olive oil
- Salt to taste
- 1 teaspoon lemon juice
- 1 egg yolk
- 1 garlic clove

Tomato Sauce Ingredients

- 2 teaspoons smoked paprika
- Salt and pepper to taste
- 1 garlic clove
- 1 red jalapeno
- 1 tablespoon olive oil
- 3 large plum tomatoes

Potato Ingredients

- 2 tablespoons olive oil
- Salt and pepper to taste
- 1 lb. potatoes

Garnish Ingredients

- Fresh lemon juice
- 1 tablespoon parsley

Method:
14. Preheat the oven to 400 degrees Fahrenheit.
15. Toss potato in canola oil and season with salt and pepper.
16. Position on a cookie sheet in a single sheet.
17. Cook for 25 to 30 minutes until its fork ready.
18. In a spice grinder, puree the vegetables to make the sauce.
19. Add the oil to a pan.
20. Garlic and jalapeno peppers should be added at this stage.
21. Insert pureed onions, cayenne pepper, salt, and pepper until the onions have softened.
22. Combine the garlic, lime juice, and egg white in a mixing dish.
23. Beat the egg yolks with an immersion blender until they are light in color.
24. Continue to beat until it thickens into a sour cream texture.
25. Mix in the salt until it is well combined.
26. Put potatoes in a dish to eat.

6.8 Spanish Vegetarian Tapas

Cooking Time: 20 minutes

Serving Size: 4

Ingredients:
- 1 tablespoon olive oil
- Fresh basil

- 1 red onion
- 1 dl mató cheese
- 1 bag of dates
- 250g small tomatoes
- 2 clove of garlic
- 2 tablespoon mató cheese
- A handful walnuts
- 1 eggplant
- 1 tablespoon maple syrup

Method:

10. Roll the dates and fill them with hazelnuts and Spanish Mató cheese.
11. Place on a tray and drizzle with maple syrup to finish.
12. Wash the tomatoes and cut them in half.
13. Parsley and red onion should be chopped.
14. Combine the tomato and Mató cheese in a mixing dish.
15. Wash the eggplant and break it into thinly sliced.
16. Grill for 2-3 minutes on each side after brushing with canola oil.
17. Cover them in foil and place them on a tray.
18. Place olive tapenade, polenta, cello, oranges, artichokes, manchego cheese, heat tomatoes, fluffy biscuits, and Spanish wine on the tapas table.

6.9 Patatas Bravas

Cooking Time: 50 minutes

Serving Size: 12

Ingredients:

For the Sauce

- Pinch sugar
- Fresh parsley
- 2 teaspoon sweet paprika
- Good pinch chili powder
- 3 tablespoon olive oil
- 227g can tomatoes
- 1 tablespoon tomato purée
- 2 garlic cloves
- 1 small onion

For the Potatoes

- 2 tablespoon olive oil
- 900g potatoes

Method:

8. In a bowl, add the oil and cook the onions for about five minutes or until hardened.
9. Bring to the boil, stirring regularly, with the garlic, diced tomatoes, vegetable purée, adobo seasoning, chili powder, cinnamon, and salt pinch.
10. Heat for ten minutes, or until the mixture is pulpy.
11. Preheat the oven to 200 degrees Celsius.

12. Fry for 40-50 minutes until it's golden brown.
13. Spoon the pasta sauce over the vegetables in spice jars.
14. To eat, garnish with grated parmesan.

6.10 Mushroom, Polenta & Tomato Tapas

Cooking Time: 30 minutes

Serving Size: 4

Ingredients:

- 4 sundried tomatoes
- Salt & pepper
- 1 clove garlic
- A small lump of parmesan
- 400g polenta
- A small handful of parsley
- A lug of olive oil
- 8 Portobello mushrooms
- 50g feta cheese
- 3 big tomatoes

Method:

9. Preheat the grill to 180 degrees Celsius.
10. Heat the polenta according to the package directions.
11. Tomatoes should be cut into rounds.
12. Remove the stems and wash the mushrooms with a towel.

13. Toss the vegetables and mushrooms in the seasoning.
14. To cook and smooth the vegetables and mushrooms, position them under the barbecue in the oven.
15. Rub the polenta round with olive oil and barbecue them on a stovetop grill, rotating to build nice lines from both ends.
16. To arrange, start with the polenta square, then a tomato slice, and finally a mushroom.

Conclusion

Tapas are far more advanced nowadays. Tapas include everything from small olive sauces to intricate culinary skills. There are also tapas competitions to see who can make the best versions! Tapas has evolved to include briny mussels, cherry tomatoes, fried cod, and other delicacies. As the tapas tradition in Spain expands, tapas bars have grown to include small plates rather than just quick bites. Tapas have become more creative in recent years, and there are now various recipes to try. Tapas was always about using new, in-season Mediterranean products as well as traditional Spanish culinary delights. That's what you'll be on the lookout for. Don't be put off by the presence of canned food in restaurants. Spain is described as having some of the finest packaged seafood on the earth. Sardines, clams, oysters, and other seafood are common in Spanish cuisine, do not be afraid to try them. Anything else would pale in comparison to the tapas culture of Spain. The excitement and the delicious food and drinks will hold you are returning for more. So give these tapas ideas a try, and you'll fall in love with the flavor of these delectable tapas.